ARTHUR E. BLOOMFIELD

The Changing Climate
by Arthur E. Bloomfield

Library of Congress Catalog Card Number 77-80427

ISBN 0-87123-060-7

Copyright © 1956, 1977
Bethany Fellowship, Inc.
All Rights Reserved

DIMENSION BOOKS
Published by Bethany Fellowship, Inc.
6820 Auto Club Road, Minneapolis, Minnesota 55438

Printed in the United States of America

ARTHUR E. BLOOMFIELD

A Methodist minister, now living in Florida, Rev. Bloomfield was a pastor for a number of years.

For six years he served as Editor of *Higley's Sunday School Commentary*.

In response to the constantly growing interest in the prophetic Scriptures, he left the pastorate to be free to devote his time more fully to their study.

Through the years he has conducted many prophetic conferences for several denominational groups, including the Christian and Missionary Alliance, Baptist, Assemblies of God, Free Lutheran, and the Evangelical United Brethren.

He is the author of seven other books, all in the area of prophecy. His best-known work is *Before the Last Battle*, a coordination of all the highlights of biblical prophecy.

He has also written *Signs of His Coming*, *The End of the Days*, *All Things New*, *Study Guide to All Things New*, *How to Recognize the Antichrist*, and *Where Is the Ark of the Covenant?*

Preface

How near are we to what the Bible calls "the end of the age"? This was an interesting question even in the time of Christ. The disciples came to Him and asked, "What shall be the sign of thy coming and the end of the age?" In His answer Jesus did not talk about the changing climate or the problem of water, but the things He talked about are connected with the disposition of water and with the climate in other portions of the Bible.

It is significant, therefore, that such things as climate and water are becoming extremely important to the human race at the same time that many other signs of the end of the age are beginning to appear.

In Genesis in the record of creation the subject of water is very prominent. On the earth it was gathered into what the Bible calls "seas," many seas, not necessarily great oceans. In Revelation, after the completed redemption of the earth, John remarked, "And there was no more sea." This book tells the story.

Arthur E. Bloomfield
Eustis, Florida

Table of Contents

Chapter 1. What Is Happening to the Weather?............................11

Chapter 2. Is the Climate Changing?............24

Chapter 3. The Bible Story 34

Chapter 4. The New Heavens and the New Earth 102

1

What Is Happening to the Weather?

Weather is the general condition of the atmosphere at a particular time and place, with regard to the temperature, moisture, cloudiness, etc. Climate is the prevailing or average weather conditions of a place, as determined by the temperature and meteorological changes over a period of years.

Within the course of a few years we have had one of the warmest winters and one of the coldest winters in history. Sometimes when the weather is unusually warm or unusually cold in one part of the world, it is the reverse in some other part. The question is: Is the overall balance of the weather changing? Authorities differ on the answer. Some claim that the climate is getting slightly warmer; others try to prove that we are heading for another ice age.

In prehistoric times the weather on the earth was so cold that great ice areas not only covered all of Canada and the Arctic Ocean but extended as far south as New York and St. Louis. Many glaciers and solid ice covered the entire North Sea, Greenland, Poland and most of Russia. What are now known as the Alps were covered by enormous glaciers.

Since the temperate zones became relatively ice free, there has been a series of cycles of warm and cold weather. The so-called little ice age reached its peak about the year 1850, and since then the glaciers have been in retreat. World climate has been slowly but steadily rising.

At first, this change was very slow and many cold winters were interspersed among the warmer ones. Then gradually the warmer winters became more frequent. As I was writing a portion of this book, I sat in a room in northern Indiana with a southern exposure. Almost every day that winter the sun, which could almost be called hot, had warmed the room. Old-timers around there told of getting out their bobsleighs at the beginning of the winter and using them all winter, two or three feet of snow being the regular thing.

For fifteen years there had been very little snow in that part of the country, and then it lasted only a short time. Those warm winters were no longer the exception. They were the regular thing; a cold winter was the exception.

The winter of 1976-1977 was the coldest in the recorded history of the United States. It remains to be seen whether this is setting a pattern, or whether we will revert to warmer winters. The authorities seem to be divided about 50-50 on this point.

According to an article in the *New York Times,* "evidence is accumulating that the ice sheets covering Antarctica, far from being permanent features, wax and wane in ways that at times must cause large changes in global sea levels." There are indications that some ice in the Antarctic is slipping seaward. This could mean a significant rise in world sea levels in the future. If this is true, the climate of the whole world could be materially affected. We probably will get some more cold winters, just as there were warm winters occasionally when the weather was, for the most part, colder.

This situation seems to be worldwide. Many Arctic ports are ice free several months of the year longer than they were a few years ago. Shipping on Hudson Bay extends over more of the year than it used to. The great birch forests of Canada have died off because of the new pests brought in by the warmer climate. One of the most convincing evidences of changing climate is found in the ocean. The fish are moving north. Many of the great fishing grounds are no longer productive.

Tropical fish have been reported caught off Long Island. The fish are moving north because the food supply is moving north. The water is getting warmer. Up until now we have thought that the change was such a slow process that it would spread over many hundreds of years, so that we would not, in our day, see any marked change, at least not one that would have disastrous effects, or change the balance of power among the countries of the world; but the facts show that, although the change has been going on for many years, the movement has suddenly begun to speed up.

This has been reflected in hundreds of reports from all over the world. For instance, during the warm cycle the United States Department of Commerce said in a bulletin entitled, "Weekly Weather and Crops": "Abnormally hot and dry weather persisted over the Southern Great Plains and Lower Mississippi Valley during the past six weeks, resulting in considerable deterioration of crops, pastures, and ranges. Temperatures for the past six weeks averaged four to ten degrees warmer than usual and maximum readings of 90 to 100 degrees occurred in an unusual number of days. Continued hot, dry weather intensified droughty conditions in many south, central and southwestern sections, while light to heavy showers and favorable temperatures maintained good to excellent crop growth in the north central regions."

In a sixteen-year period the sardine industry on the Pacific Coast dwindled to almost nothing from a $65,000,000 industry. Tuna fish and salmon are going to become very scarce unless some new fishing methods are devised. Salmon around Alaska prefer to stay out in the ocean where the water is cold rather than to come in near shore to get caught. Everywhere ocean fish are on the move. Something is happening.

Not only are the fish moving north but so are trees, plants, vegetables—and bugs. Wheat is being raised farther north in Canada than ever before, and corn is being grown in the southern part of Canada. Some countries, such as Canada and Russia will profit greatly by this changing climate; but other countries are less fortunate. Some will be almost ruined.

One of the most serious effects of the changing climate is the rainfall, or lack of it, in many areas. The western part of the United States may suffer greatly, and some countries may be brought to a state of catastrophe. This is probably caused by the fact that changing climate means changing winds.

Over quite a large area, the wells are dry or threatening to go dry. There have been no snows in the winter to melt and replenish the water in the ground. The water table is lowering. In other places high water has been almost disastrous. The Great Lakes are higher than normal, and Niagara Falls has more water going over it than ever before. These conditions will not get better if the present trend continues. Snow is melting on the tops of the mountains where, for hundreds of years, it has been accumulating. Up until now more snow has fallen every winter than has melted in the summer. Now more snow is melting in the summer than falls in the winter, so there is going to be high water in some places and little water in others.

Meteorologists have estimated that a rise of only

two degrees in the earth's temperature would melt all the ice of the polar seas and increase the height of the ocean level by 150 feet, and that a rise of four degrees in world temperature would be disastrous for mankind.

There are many factors which go into the matter of temperature, and there are many causes of the change. Some of them are in outer space. The sun, for instance, could affect the temperature of the earth only slightly, yet enough to start the cycle of change.

The sun gives the earth heat without heating intervening space. Actually, the sun does not radiate heat at all; it radiates rays of energy which are transformed into heat after they reach the vicinity of the earth. This transformation is produced by the atmosphere and by the earth itself. Ice and snow do not transform the sun's rays into heat; neither do trees. Trees help to cool the air. Every tree is a natural air-conditioning unit.

On the other hand, the deserts are the earth's furnaces. They produce the greater part of the heat. The rocks, the stones, the bare ground are also furnaces. When conditions become such that the snow and the ice begin to melt faster than they accumulate, that, in itself, will produce more and more warm climate, because that makes more and more heating equipment for the earth. In turn, that melts more ice and snow, and again more heat-producing earth is uncovered; and so, after a while the process is accelerated to the extent that it becomes very noticeable. From that time on, the acceleration will tend to increase every year. At the same time that this is going on in the northern countries, the lack of water in other places, where water is normally scarce, makes for more deserts. In Africa, for instance, the deserts are reported to be growing in extent, and the dry parts of this country will tend to return to desert unless new sources of water can be found. That increases the amount of heat produced on the earth.

Here we have a chain reaction which gives us the reason why the change will come faster and faster every year after a certain point, and that point we seem to have reached.

This whole process could have been started by man himself cutting down large forest areas and turning them into cultivation. It is like tearing down air-conditioning plants and turning them into furnaces. This, in itself, might be enough to start the cycle. At first, of course, it would not be noticeable, and then suddenly it would reach a point where the world's climate would change so fast that people could not change with it and great shifts of population would be the result.

It should be noted, however, that most scientists have agreed that the sun itself is not exactly steady and that a great change in temperature is probably the result of more energy being received from the sun.

Reports are appearing in the newspapers that Russia is planning to change the course of two rivers that now flow into the Arctic Ocean, as a means of changing the climate of northern Russia so that they can grow more wheat. Fresh water freezes at a higher temperature than salt water. To prevent the flow of so much fresh water into the ocean would cause less ice to be formed, and this would raise the temperature slightly. This is an illustration of how man could innocently start a revolution in the climate that would eventually affect the entire earth. No one can predict the future climate of the earth because no one can predict what man will do.

This book first appeared in 1956. At that time there was in effect a cycle of extra warm weather. In 1976-

1977 there was a return to cold weather in some parts of the earth. This was local in nature, and does not affect materially the overall climate of the earth which many scientists believe is getting warmer. In 1956 there were evidences that the world was getting warmer. This does not mean that there will be no more cold winters. The overall climate of the earth does not depend upon the weather of a certain part of the earth at a given time, but on the average of the whole earth over a period of years.

For instance, back in 1956 a news release from Washington said man-made satellites might help to determine why the world was getting warmer.

> The Weather Bureau disclosed that it is joining in the attempt to send a man-made satellite above the earth in hope of finding out why the world is getting warmer.
>
> Weather Bureau chief Francis W. Reichelderfer said some scientists suspect temperatures are going up because the sun may be giving out more heat than it did a generation or so ago.
>
> He said in an interview:
>
> "There are indications that the temperatures throughout the world are one or two or three degrees warmer than they were 10 or 20 years ago. At least we suspect that's true although we don't have complete records for all parts of the earth.
>
> "Actually that doesn't mean that summers are becoming warmer—although this summer may change our minds about that.
>
> "It means that winters are not as cold as they once were."
>
> Reichelderfer said this was one of the reasons the Weather Bureau is "quite enthusiastic" about the daring plan to launch a satellite which will circle the earth at an altitude of 200 miles and a speed of 18,000 miles an hour.
>
> He explained: "We don't really know whether

this warming up is due to a change in output of radiation from the sun—whether the stove is getting hotter—or whether it is due to some change in the composition of the upper atmosphere through which the sun's rays must pass or both."

The weathermen believe that instruments aboard the unmanned spacecraft will send back information that can help unlock some of these mysteries. Reichelderfer said his bureau has been in on the secret planning for the project and "will certainly participate in the meteorological aspects."

Most people do not realize the enormous amount of water that is stored up in the Arctic and Antarctic regions in the form of ice and snow. We sometimes think of the North Pole and the South Pole as being small areas. Our maps show them that way.

Antarctica is a tremendous continent having 6,000,000 square miles of ice and snow, and the Arctic stores up a tremendous amount of water in the form of ice. For centuries the snow has been falling on those regions and staying there, forming great icecaps. On Greenland there is an icecap extending over 700,000 square miles, and in places it is a mile and a half high. It is beginning to melt.

If this ice should melt, it would change the complexion of the whole earth. Should this change come over a period of thousands of years, the population of the earth would adapt itself to it, but if it should come quickly over a period of only a few years, the results would be such as are almost impossible to contemplate.

There is more water at the poles than there ought to be. There is too much water on the earth, and there is plenty of evidence in the earth, as well as in the Bible, that the water came suddenly to the earth. It is certain that the poles were once warm. The forms of tropical plants have been found buried in the ice at the South Pole, and as the ice melts in the far north, animals are being uncovered that have been kept in a deep freeze these thousands of years, their flesh so well preserved that dogs will eat it. This indicates that the change from hot to cold came suddenly.

Only quick freezing would preserve the plants and animals as they have been preserved. These animals and plants were used to warm weather, and then suddenly they were frozen and buried in tons of ice and snow. For the past 60 years this ice has been noticeably melting, but very slowly. Now the rate of melting has been suddenly speeded up, so that the results are becoming very pronounced.

Back in 1956 I had the privilege of talking to some missionaries to the Eskimos in northern Canada. The Eskimos live by hunting and fishing. The caribou, arctic deer, furnish their livelihood. They eat the flesh and wear the skins.

The missionaries told me that the caribou are moving north because of the changing climate and many Eskimos are left destitute. They said also that they could use boats on Hudson Bay a month longer than formerly.

I met a man from Norway who told me that his people were in a bad way because the fishing grounds were empty. Norway depends upon fishing and the fish are moving to other waters. The fishermen cannot always follow the fish because they move into Russian-controlled waters.

Many fish are becoming Communists and are refusing to return to be caught by Capitalist fishermen. England is experiencing similar trouble. The big question is: Is this change in climate something temporary, just a few years of unusual weather, or is it a real threat to the world? One answer may be found in the ocean. The ocean water is definitely becoming warmer. A few years of warm weather would not cause the ocean fish to change their habits so radically. It is more fundamental than that.

This is dramatically illustrated by the changing picture in Norway. There a big boom is under way because of the warm-water fish that are moving into Norwegian waters, especially tuna. Warming the water just a few degrees has enriched the marine life and the fish follow the food sources.

Birds were also changing their habits. I was in Minneapolis that spring for a Bible conference, and I noticed the large number of robins on the lawns. The robins were going farther north.

From Michigan came this report:

> There's a multitude of bugs that we never saw before. One cheerful note is the multitude of birds. They are more plentiful every year. They eat some fruit but keep us from utter destruction by the bugs. The robins are in the majority. One time I counted thirty-six on our lawn at once, and several were flying about that I could not count. Some stay all winter. We also have opossum. They have only been here in recent years, so I am told.

Animals are quick to note a change in climate. Opossum cannot stand cold winters. They have seldom wandered north of Virginia. Now they are becoming common in northern Indiana. Other southern animals may be expected to follow.

Pests are also coming in from the south. In 1955 in Indiana I had more trouble raising a garden. More pests and more kinds of pests appeared. I sprayed more but, in spite of that, lost much of the crop. The bugs ate everything. In that locality there are a large number of manufacturers of house trailers. They had been using birch for the interiors. Scrap birch had been plentiful and many people used it in their houses or for making novelties and shelves. Then it was becoming scarce. The trailer companies were importing plywood from Japan instead. Upon inquiry I found that the birch forests in Canada were dying off like the chestnut trees did many years ago. The French-Canadian Society for the Advancement of Science said that the dying out of the birch tree was the worst calamity ever to hit the Province of Quebec, which lost 30 million cords of birchwood due to the blight. Birch trees simply could not stand the warm weather, or rather, they could not survive the pests that the warm weather brought.

On the other hand in Canada, Sweden, Finland, Russia and Alaska many trees were growing in areas where they had never grown before: such trees as the pine, willow, ash, spruce and maple.

These things could not result from two or three freak winters. Something was happening to the world that had not happened before in the memory of man.

Something else was happening at the same time which must be considered as a part of the process. The earth's crust was rising in the north causing the water to flow south. That is probably the reason why the Great Lakes were so high. There were reports from Long Island and other places along the Atlantic Coast of high water washing away land and property and flooding houses.

The missionaries to the Eskimos, referred to earlier, told me that Hudson Bay was getting lower so that new islands and reefs were appearing. As the ice melted and ran south, the north areas were relieved of the tremendous weight; and the crust of the earth, which had been compressed all those years, tended to rise.

This would help to increase the amount of water in the temperate zones. It also might cause "earthquakes in divers places."

In May 1952, The American Academy of Arts and Sciences held a two-day conference on the subject of climate change, where about twenty specialists in the various fields of investigation touching upon climate were assembled. It resulted in a book containing twenty-two papers on the subject. This book was edited by Harlow Shapely, famous astronomer, and published by the Harvard University Press. It is not easy for the layman to read. Here is one of the simpler sentences: "There is continually in progress an entire spectrum of cyclical fluctuations of climate, cycles of shorter period and smaller amplitude being superimposed on those of longer period and larger amplitude."

The chapter by Harlow Shapely dealing mostly with the possibility of life on other planets is fairly easy to read. He says: "Actually the warming of the Arctic has been going on, the glacial and biological records indicate, for about forty years. Arctic Meteorology deserves and is now receiving much attention in the interests of today's weather and yesterday's climate."

A much easier book to understand was written by William J. Baxter and published by the International Economic Research Bureau of New York City. He reduced the highly scientific terms of the experts to plain and sometimes humorous language; but his conclusions were the same.

Both books, for instance, quote Professor Huntington of Yale who showed conclusively that a rise of only four degrees in temperature would have disastrous consequences. It would rapidly melt all the accumulated ice on this planet and flood such cities as New York,

Philadelphia and Boston, and sometimes whole countries.

High water is not the only result of the melting ice. The polar ice has a great effect on the temperature of the country. The winter winds blow from the north bringing in cold and snow. As the ice melts the winds become warmer, or they may change their direction altogether, bringing more rainfall in some places and less in others. Some parts of the United States, now cultivated, may return to desert.

2
Is the Climate Changing?

Summary of Unusual Weather Features

One of the most striking facts of the circulation during July 1954 was the persistence of weather type over many regions of the Northern Hemisphere. The results of this persistence were widely noted and deserve mention.

Great Britain experienced cold and stormy weather with only very brief interludes of more pleasant conditions. Central Europe was similarly plagued. Since June weather also had been stormy in Europe, 70 continuous hours of rain and snow on the Alps in early July sent the Danube well over its banks. This flood was characterized as the worst in centuries. At one time the river flooded a stretch of some 300 miles from Vienna upstream. As the crest passed downstream both Vienna (July 14) and Budapest were hard hit and surrounding farm lands were inundated.

Late July floods were also reported from Iran and from East Pakistan and eastern India, but these were dwarfed by the accounts of Chinese disasters. Apparently wide areas of China were deluged with rain in early July, and the rising waters congregating in the 3,100-mile-long Yangtze River left widespread destruction.

Hundreds of miles of the Yangtze Valley were flooded, and a new all-time high water mark was recorded at Wuhan as late as mid-August.

In contrast to the cold and floods so prominent elsewhere, the United States was troubled by heat and drought. Their greatest effects were felt in the six-state area: Nebraska, Kansas, Oklahoma, Louisiana, Missouri, and Arkansas, as well as northern and western portions of Texas. Above normal temperatures were both persistent and extreme—on the 14th St. Louis recorded 115 degrees F. and East St. Louis, 117 degrees F., the highest temperature ever recorded on or east of the Mississippi River. Deficient rainfall combined with searing heat compounded the drought conditions remaining from June.—*Monthly Weather Review*—U.S. Govt.

This, with slight variations, could be repeated for 1955.

It is high time, in the opinion of Greenland-born Dr. Svend Frederiksen of Washington's Arctic Institute, that the world take account of its changing climate. For 50 years or more, says Dr. Frederiksen, the climate of the Arctic has been warming up, making agriculture possible where it has not been practiced in modern times.

"Already," he says, "we are deep in the warming-up period."

The world must be getting a little warmer, according to Meteorologist Victor T. Horn of the U.S. Weather Bureau in Government Square.

He pointed out that a revision of daily average temperatures for the period from 1920 to 1950 upped the lowest for the winter season by two degrees, as well as changing the period for the minimum.

It used to be that Parkersburg's lowest winter average was 32 degrees, based on figures prior to 1920, and occurred for a few days around February 10. Under the revised table the minimum is 34 degrees and occurs from January 16 to 20.

Warmer summers have started a forest revolution in northern New England and eastern Canada. Dr. Rene Pomerleau, director of Canada's forest pathology laboratory at Laval University, Quebec, estimates that at least one half of all the birch trees in the area have been killed over the past twenty years by a three-degree rise in average temperature. Hotter summers, accentuated by wanton cutting of virgin forests, have already baked and killed the shallow roots of some 25 million cubic feet of timber. The future of the region's trees depends on whether this planet's warmup is permanent —a meteorological row Dr. Pomerleau refuses to enter—but he has other evidence that spruce, balsam, and even maples are also beginning to feel the change.

On the other hand, in 1977 just the reverse conditions obtained in the United States; the whole country was colder than normal, and there was a serious lack of snow in the West. This might be a natural fluctuation in one small part of the earth with little bearing on the overall climatic change.

Man's chimneys and combustion engines are sending about 12 billion tons of carbon dioxide a year into the earth's atmosphere. In the next 50 years, this rate may quadruple. Such an increase, by trapping more heat, may raise the earth's average temperature by one degree or two degrees F.—and that, in turn, might over an extended period of time melt the Greenland icecap and the vast Antarctic ice fields, raise the level of the oceans by 170 feet, swamp every port and seacoast in the world and push the shore of the Gulf of Mexico north to Memphis, Tennessee.

Cyclones

Cyclones in increasing numbers and coming farther inland are one of the more noticeable results of the changing climate. The winds are changing. This is another result of climatic change, for the winds are produced and guided largely by differences in temperature. The effects of the changing winds are drought in some parts of the country, floods in others, and cyclones and tornados in unusual places.

High Water

Water is high in the South Pole areas and low in the North Pole areas—another way of saying land is rising in the north and sinking in the south. On the Atlantic seaboard New York seems to be the dividing point at present. This point was brought out in the article in the *Saturday Evening Post* in the "U.S. Geographical Survey" by Harold H. Martin:

> The West Coast right now is rising slowly and tilting toward the East; and the East Coast, south of New York, is slowly sinking. Nobody knows why. North of New York the land is rising, but there is a reason for that. The earth that was pressed down under the great weight of the glaciers is slowly regaining its original shape.

This accounts for the rising of the land north of New York. The reason for the sinking of the land or the rising of the water south of New York may be found in the report coming from the South Pole area. Our government sent a new expedition to visit the South Pole along with the previous British expeditions which were sent there because of the reports of the sinking land, disappearing islands and melting ice. The reports coming from the South Pole indicate that the temperature is rising—the ice is melting at an alarming rate. The high water would be only temporary if the ice did not continue to melt; as water seeks its own level, the ocean would level off, and the rise would be very slight, but if the ice continues to melt at the same or at an increasingly faster rate, then the water will remain high for a long time in the south.

The following was taken from press reports published in England.

> It is reported from Santiago: During the big gale sweeping the west coast of the southernmost tip of South America and Tierra del Fuego in October 1950, for four days, three middle-sized islands disappeared into the Pacific Ocean without a trace. Since then the Chilean geologists are in no doubt that the group of islands and flat coastal strips near the Strait of Magellan will gradually disappear into the sea.
>
> An expert opinion from Santiago says that the unusually warm gale roaring from the direction of the South Pole initiated a shifting of the weather zones. Since then an increased melting of the South Polar Icecap has to be reckoned with.
>
> Statements to the same effect, and at the same time, by American geologists were given as little credence in world publicity as the declarations of their Chilean colleagues.
>
> However, since the large island, Magallanes, has been flooded for over three months and the floods of the Pacific Ocean are continuing to rise, a British expedition and an American one have gone to Punta Arenas, to find out on the spot whether or not the west coast of South America does sink into the sea.
>
> Immediately after the arrival of the expeditionary ship "Mary," the British geologist, Professor Shursbore, sent a cable to his London colleague, Dr. Graham: "Outwork Punta Arenas stands ten feet under wa-

ter. No prospect of sea level receding. Am deeply shaken about carelessness and lack of interest of world publicity about this extraordinary rise of the ocean. Explanation definitely to be sought in melting processes of Antarctic ice."

The British escort vessel "Titan" had meanwhile reached the South Pole ice barrier, cabling from there to Punta Arenas:

"Shipping lane nearly free of ice floes and pack ice as far as central ice zone. Within a few years enormous quantities of Antarctic ice must have melted. Intensive investigations urgently required. Temperature in central ice district four degrees higher than two years ago."

These reports have caused understandable excitement in scientific circles, especially as the ice masses of the North Pole and of Greenland have likewise begun to melt.

The ocean will level off with a rise of only a small fraction of an inch, but a new warming spell would again bring a temporary rise in the water around the Antarctic. These are not permanent conditions now, but they show a trend that, as we shall see, could suddenly begin to accelerate at great speed. Our concern now is that the Bible has much to say about this very thing.

The U.S. Government also sent expeditions into the Antarctic. A preliminary expedition of one ship, the Atka, reported that large portions of the Ross Ice Barrier have broken away and that unusually warm weather prevailed while they were there. (*Saturday Evening Post*, July 23, 1955)

Melting Ice May Submerge Florida

It may be nothing to worry about, but at least one government scientist thinks Florida may be submerged at some time in the future.

He's Dr. L. M. Gould, member of the U.S. National Committee for the International Geophysical Year, National Academy of Sciences and National Research Council.

Supporting a request for research funds for use in the Antarctic, Gould told a House Appropriations subcommittee:

"We know since 1900 that the climate or weather of the polar region has been warming up at an unprecedented rate. If it goes on at the present rate, in 25 or 50 years we will be using the Arctic Ocean for navigation.

"I do not believe the Antarctic icecap will melt enough to worry you and me, but if all the ice started to melt at some time in the future, it would submerge Florida. But we know so little: that is the reason the Antarctic item is so important."—Newspaper

The U.S. Coast and Geodetic Survey report shows what has been happening to the coastline during the last 40 or 50 years. In that time the ocean has risen about six inches, but the greater part of that rise has come in the last few years. It is rising faster every year. (New York, at Battery Park, is only four feet above sea level.)

Insects

New insects appear every year causing great damage to crops and to trees. These insects are not new to the world; they are just new to the areas that are warming up. The insects follow the climate changes. People change slowly; their habits are more or less fixed. It will be some time before people in great numbers change their habits, but insects can change year by year with the changing climate. Insect plagues will be more and more a factor in the north until measures are perfected to bring them under control.

Fish

Fish move with the food supply. If the waters are getting warmer in the north, food will grow in those waters and the fish will follow. Reports of such changes in fish population are coming from all salt waters. This indicates not a temporary change but a more or less permanent or growing one.

Vegetation

A representative of a Bible institute in Canada told me that the seasons are changing. Snowfall comes a month or more later then formerly, and the winter lasts longer into the spring. However, the overall temperature has been much higher than normal the past few years and seems to be getting warmer. He said that they were being told that the time was coming when they would be growing citrus fruits around their institute. Corn is being raised successfully much farther north than ever before. This may be due in part to the improved strains of corn that can stand the colder climates, but it is partly due to the fact that the weather is decidedly warmer in Canada than it ever has been since that territory was settled. General farm crops are being grown as far north as Great Slave Lake, and cabbages and potatoes are grown as far north as the Arctic Red River and Great Bear Lake. Good vegetables, except corn, are being grown successfully almost to the Yukon.

The tree lines also are creeping north across all of Canada; at the same time, the birch forests are dying off in the southern part of Canada, due to the pests brought in by warmer weather.

Vegetables that were considered southern crops are now being grown almost to the Canadian border—such as sweet potatoes, peanuts and watermelons.

Air Conditioning

Air conditioning is one of the fastest growing industries in the north as well as in the south. Excessive heat for long periods of time saps the energy from workers and makes a big difference in the output. Manufacturers are faced with the necessity of moving farther north or air-conditioning their entire plants. Air-conditioning units for homes are having a big sale.

Longer Hot Spells

During the past few summers very few records were broken by the heat. Sometime in the past there has been an extra hot day almost every date on the calendar. However, the difference is that the hot spells last longer than they used to. In the past years we have had possibly a week or so of unusually hot weather at a time. Now we have nearly a record-breaking heat spell for a month at a time; then after a few days of relief another long hot spell comes.

In some parts of the world this is not so. England and Germany are noticing cooler weather, sometimes even cold weather, during the summer. This, however, has the same cause. The heat causes the winds to change, and also the Gulf Stream, so that the tendency is for Europe to become colder at the same time that the United States is becoming warmer. This does not affect the overall temperature of the earth because the critical point is the freezing point, and the overall temperature of the earth hovers close to the freezing point. A degree or two, one way or the other, is the difference between water and ice. The earth is about at that point now so that only two or three degrees difference in temperature marks the difference between cold climate and the warm climate of the greater part of the earth. Although the temperature in Europe may be cooler during the summer, it does not have any effect on the freezing or the melting of the ice. It does not get that cold.

If only one or two of these items were involved, there might be some other explanation, but when every phase of life, in the sea, or the earth, and in the air, are all feeling the same change at the same time; then we can be very sure something is happening. Just one or two extra mild winters, or extra hot summers, would not warm up the water so that the fish would change their habits. The same is true of the birds and the insects and the trees.

We have taken 1956 as a typical year. Of course, conditions are continually changing; there will be some extra cold winters and summers interspersed. After all, a rise of two or three degrees would hardly be noticed. This is a long-term process unless man does something with his many new tools to speed it up. News items coming out of Russia would indicate that Russia is very much alive to the possibilities.

A feverish investigation of the heavens is now going on for the express purpose of studying the weather and its causes. This is much more important for Russia than for the United States. Breaking up the Arctic ice would open thousands of square miles of new fertile land for Russia at the same time that it would wash out the largest cities in the United States.

Russia knows this. A news item quoted from a Russian paper says that the Russians know how to make Siberia as warm as France. This may be Russia's most powerful weapon.

3
The Bible Story of Water

The surface of the earth is about three quarters water and one quarter land. The proportion of water would be much greater if all the ice at the poles should melt. The polar icecap is high, sometimes as much as a mile. On Greenland it reaches to a mile and a half.

It is estimated that if all this ice should melt, it would raise the ocean level by 150 feet. This would cover with water another large portion of land. Not only would such islands as Magallanes disappear, but Long Island and Manhattan Island would be no more.

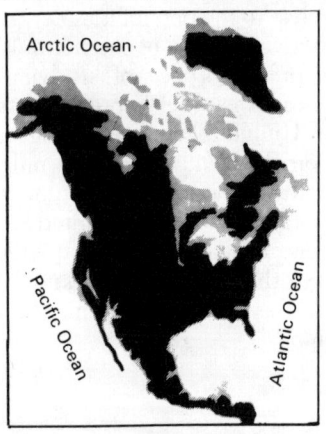

Map shows how coastline of North America would be affected by 180 foot rise in sea level.

Water, just plain water, can be a greater threat to the world than Communism. We might defeat Communism by a war, but there is no power of man that can defeat the threat of flood when God releases the surplus water. Only God can stop that disaster. He will stop it. The Bible tells how.

Now we are confronted with two arresting facts:

(1) There was a time when there was no extra water at the poles, and at that time the poles were warm.

(2) There was, at about the same time, much less water on the earth, so there was a much greater proportion of land. It is believed that islands in the ocean were once connected with the mainland.

In other words, there was a time when this surplus water was not on the earth at all. Much of the water now in the ocean must be considered as surplus water. That brings us to an interesting question.

The New Heaven and the New Earth

What was the earth like when God created it? We are not told in Genesis how much of the surface of the earth was land and how much was water, but we do know that God intends to regenerate the earth.

Matthew 19

28 And Jesus said unto them, Verily I say unto you, That ye which have followed me, in the regeneration, when the Son of man shall sit in the throne of his glory, ye also shall sit upon twelve thrones, judging the twelve tribes of Israel.

Regeneration—palingenesia—a new genesis, a re-creation. In Titus 3:5, the only other place where the word is used, regeneration refers to the new birth, but here the reference is to the created order, the earth.

Revelation 21
5 Behold, I make all things new

is the most concise statement of God's purpose.

Isaiah 65

17 For, behold, I create new heavens and a new earth: and the former shall not be remembered, nor come into mind.

This redeemed heaven and earth is the subject of much Bible prophecy and we can, therefore, know something about it. Regeneration is the restoration to the original state. Redemption is the restoration to the original owner. The earth is to be regenerated and redeemed. The word "redemption" usually includes regeneration. We may learn something about the original heaven and earth by a look at the restored heaven and earth.

When John saw this new earth, one physical feature stood out so strongly that it impressed him above all others. It was the only one he mentioned: "And there was no more sea."

Revelation 21

1 And I saw a new heaven and a new earth: for the first heaven and the first earth were passed away; and there was no more sea.

This is retrospect. John was summing up. He had seen the world as it is today. He had seen the destruction of the Day of the Lord—the earthquakes, the falling stars, the fire and the hail. He had seen every wall fall to the ground and the mountains moved, bringing whole new continents into being. He had seen the surplus water disappear.

There is no suggestion here, nor anywhere else in the Bible, that God is going to wipe this planet out of existence and put another one in its place. The earth is "without end."

Isaiah 45

17 But Israel shall be saved in the Lord with an

everlasting salvation: ye shall not be ashamed nor confounded world without end.

18 For thus saith the Lord that created the heavens; God himself that formed the earth and made it; he hath established it, he created it not in vain, he formed it to be inhabited: I am the Lord; and there is none else.

The kingdom to be established here on this earth at the coming of Christ is an everlasting kingdom. Of His kingdom there shall be no end.

"Passed away" is a redemptive expression. Paul, after his conversion, said:

II Corinthians 5

17 Therefore if any man be in Christ, he is a new creature: old things are passed away; behold, all things are become new.

When the regeneration of the earth is complete, then old things have passed away and all things have become new. This is expressed exactly in:

Revelation 21

4 And God shall wipe away all tears from their eyes; and there shall be no more death, neither sorrow, nor crying, neither shall there be any more pain: for the former things are passed away.

Isaiah also expresses this thought:

Isaiah 65

17 For, behold, I create new heavens and a new earth: and the former shall not be remembered, nor come into mind.

The former heaven and earth will go into the past and be forgotten—that is the meaning of "passed away." They will be completely changed, regenerated, restored to their original perfection. The balance of the chapter makes this abundantly clear:

Isaiah 65

25 The wolf and the lamb shall feed together, and the lion shall eat straw like the bullock: and dust shall be the serpent's meat. They shall not hurt nor destroy in all my holy mountain, saith the Lord.

This perfecting of the earth is a gradual process. It is the result of the thousand-year reign of Christ and the saints. This is also brought to light in:

Isaiah 65

18 But be ye glad and rejoice for ever in that which I create: for, behold, I create Jerusalem a rejoicing, and her people a joy.

19 And I will rejoice in Jerusalem, and joy in my people: and the voice of weeping shall be no more heard in her, nor the voice of crying.

20 There shall be no more thence an infant of days, nor an old man that hath not filled his days: for the child shall die an hundred years old; but the sinner being an hundred years old shall be accursed.

This is not the final state, but the process toward it. It is that which will obtain in the millennial reign. It is the process toward perfection where there is no death. It is the way God creates the new earth. When it is all over, John can look back and say: "The former things are passed away. There is a new heaven and a new earth."

The Storehouse of Water

This is not the first time there was a new heaven and a new earth. Genesis recounts the making of a new earth. This was also a remaking, as the earth has been here for a long time. We may learn something of the restored heaven and earth by looking at the former one.

Genesis 1

6 And God said, Let there be a firmament in the midst of the waters, and let it divide the waters from the waters.

7 And God made the firmament and divided the waters which were under the firmament from the waters which were above the firmament: and it was so.

8 And God called the firmament Heaven. And the evening and the morning were the second day.

9 And God said, Let the waters under the heaven be gathered together unto one place, and let the dry land appear: and it was so.

10 And God called the dry land Earth; and the gathering together of the waters called he Seas: and God saw that it was good.

The word for seas, in both the Hebrew and the Greek, may be used of bodies of water large or small. The meaning must be gathered from the context. The original seas could have been large, large enough for whales, and still not be larger than the Mediterranean. On the other hand, there could have been a great number of them, all connected. Whole new continents could rise in the oceans and still there would be plenty of water.

When John said: "There was no more sea," he could have meant that the great oceans were filled with new expanses of land so that we would have the "seas" of Genesis rather than the "sea" or ocean of the present time.

If, then, there was less water, at the first, and more dry land, where was this extra water? Genesis tells us. The firmament, called Heaven, is the sky—the atmosphere above the earth. This firmament was in the midst of the waters so that it divided the waters from the waters. Genesis suggests that the division was somewhat equal. There was a great amount of water above the sky. This water that was above the sky was not then upon the earth. Instead of being three quarters water and one quarter land, the surface of the earth might have been more land than water. The animals that God created could easily have migrated to all parts of the earth where their remains have been found.

Even the remote islands of the sea could have been connected to mainland, as must have been the case. Great changes have taken place on the earth since those days of re-creation.

But what about the water above the firmament? There is no such water there now. Water at that height would be almost transparent. The sun, moon and stars could be seen, although possibly not with the same clarity.

Dr. Vail, one of the scientists who first brought out this theory of water around the earth, thought that this water was in the form of a ring somewhat like the rings around Saturn, only wider. The rings, he thought, were wide enough to produce the sifting of the cosmic rays, but not wide enough to hide the entire sky. However, this ring theory is not necessary to conform to Genesis. Water in some forms is quite transparent. Hot steam is transparent, so are some forms of vapor. Pure water itself is quite transparent at a distance.

But life on the earth would be quite different. Life would be impossible now if it were not for the layer of strange gas that sifts out certain lethal rays from the sun. Water would sift out other rays, possibly those which allow decay and fermentation. Life would be much longer. Food would not spoil as quickly. The temperature would probably be evener and the light softer. Such a water canopy might have the effect of air conditioning, making the whole earth a paradise.

This seems to have been the condition between the time of the Garden of Eden and the Flood. The canopy of water above the firmament would provide a vast amount of water needed for the Flood. Rain clouds, as we know them today, would not be a sufficient source of water for a flood that covered the earth to the tops of the mountains.

Clouds are formed by the evaporation of water so the total amount remains constant, but at the Flood the amount of water on the earth was suddenly increased. This extra water seems to have come from two sources.

Genesis 7

11 In the six hundredth year of Noah's life, in the second month, the seventeenth day of the month, the same day were all the fountains of the great deep broken up, and the windows of heaven were opened.

Dr. Vail thought the great deep was the reservoir of water above the earth. In that case the breaking up of the great deep and the opening of the windows of heaven would be the same thing.

However, water may have come from two directions, up from the ground and down from the heavens. The water that came out of the ground may have gone back into the ground after the Flood. The water that came down from the sky did not return, but evidently rushed to the poles. Some remained so that large amounts of land never appeared again, but remained under water, and will so remain as long as this surplus water stays on the earth.

There must have been an enormous tidal wave when that flood water rushed to the polar regions of the earth. It would certainly have swept back around the earth if it had not been instantly stopped and held there by freezing.

Now we are told that the poles were once warm and that they froze suddenly. As the icecap melts, animals are being uncovered which have been in a deep freeze these thousands of years. Some of them still have grass in their mouths and are preserved so well that dogs will eat the flesh. Only quick freezing would so preserve them.

Now we have this as a certainty: The poles were warm. Warm weather animals lived there. Vegetation was abundant. The poles suddenly froze. When the poles froze, the animals were encased in ice. The freezing was simultaneous with the coming of the water.

We also know that the reason the poles are cold is that the earth is inclined on its axis by 23 1/2 degrees. If the earth were parallel to the sun at all times, the poles would be warm.

If, therefore, the poles suddenly became cold, and if that cold has caused the "tipping" of the earth, then the earth must have tipped suddenly. This could have been caused by the rush of water to the poles. In fact, it must have been caused by the rush of water to the poles if the animals there are imbedded in the ice.

When the earth suddenly tipped, it suddenly got dark at the poles, and remained dark for six months of the year. This is all expressed so eloquently in Job.

Job 38

8 Or who shut up the sea with doors, when it brake forth, as if it had issued out of the womb?

9 When I made the cloud the garment thereof, and thick darkness a swaddling band for it,

10 And established my decree upon it [margin], and set bars and doors,

11 And said, Hitherto shalt thou come, but no further: and here shall thy proud waves be stayed?

This has been applied to Genesis, when God separated the waters into seas. But there is no indication there of any such turmoil or breaking forth with a mighty rush. There were no clouds in the Genesis story. In fact, it says that it had not rained upon the earth, but a mist went up and watered the land. There is no mention of rain till the Flood.

That canopy of water surrounding the earth might have had some surprising effects, especially as the sun set, producing a refracted light of gorgeous colors. Even now we can sometimes see the sun after it has set if the atmosphere is just right. The rays are bent by the water in the sky. A complete canopy of water might bring a long twilight. Maybe it never would get absolutely dark. But when the sky cleared and the earth tipped, thick darkness prevailed. God made the thick darkness a swaddlingband, as He told Job.

He established the water in a decreed place and set bars and doors of ice to hold it there.

Greenland is about four times the size of France. It is blanketed by a cover of 700,000 square miles of ice. It has been melting in the past at the rate of about 25 cubic miles a year. At this rate it would take about 30,000 years for Greenland to become all green.

Newsweek says that if a series of atomic explosions should destroy this icecap and turn it into water, it would raise the level of the ocean all over the world by 23 feet, inundating all the world's seaports.

According to *Newsweek* Paul-Emile Victor, a former U.S. Air Force captain who has specialized in Arctic work, says that this Greenland icecap should not be there. Heat generated by the earth's surface and by the motion of the glaciers should have melted it thousands of years ago, along with the other glaciers now extinct. Now here is a marvelous thing—ice enough to flood the seaports of the world stored up in one place where it should not be! According to the working out of the laws of nature, that ice should have melted long ago; yet it is still there held by some mysterious force, for a purpose not so mysterious because it has been revealed. God told Job that He had shut up the sea with bars and doors and established a decree upon it, and said: "Hitherto shalt thou come, but no further: and here shall thy proud waves be stayed."

However, God does not depend upon atom bombs to break up the ice. He has ways and means of His own.

God has plans for this earth. He intends to redeem it and to restore it to its original state or something better. That water is not to remain at the poles forever. The ice will melt; and when it does, we have arrived at the beginning of the time in history that all the prophets looked forward to. God will first use the water, and then put it back where it was.

In parts of Alaska the ice never melts. It is the land of the permafrost. Buildings are built on this solid foundation. Several years ago a newspaper report told of a very costly government building which had stood for years on this permanent ice and was beginning to fall over. The ice had melted on one side.

Another newspaper report told of Eskimos rushing to the beaches and to the soda fountains to cool off because they could not stand the 90-degree temperature. It was supposed to be a humorous story, but it will not be funny if it continues a few more years.

Of course, the question still is: Is this an actual trend or only a few mild winters and hot summers that just happen to come along? But, as stated above, scientists have been watching this change for about forty years. What we have experienced in the last few years is only the culmination of what has been going on for forty years. If that is true, then we may expect a faster acceleration, warmer and warmer climate, and the warmer climate reaching farther north.

It is an endless chain, always accelerating. Warmer weather melts some ice. Less ice means warmer weather because it is the ice that makes the cold weather. So, once the cycle starts it grows, always increasing in degree of change. It is like a chain reaction. The cycle seems to have started. It has reached almost the point where it cannot stop.

It is not an accident that it has come at this time. Science has reached a point where it can produce instruments that would destroy the earth and bring conditions worse than the seven last plagues. But Jesus said that would be a time of trouble such as never was, or ever would be again. That time of trouble is a judgment from heaven.

It is God's plan to redeem the earth; it is Satan's plan to destroy the earth. Satan now has this power in the new weapons of war. The question soon will be: Which will come first, Satan's destruction or God's redemption? It will be Satan's destruction unless God acts first. It may be that God is beginning to act. He has planned for this situation and has reserved the ice and snow for His own use when the day comes— J-Day, Judgment Day.

When the waters of the Flood came upon the earth, God locked them up at the poles and held them there against "that day." God said to Job:

Job 38

8 Or who shut up the sea with doors, when it brake forth, as if it had issued out of the womb?

9 When I made the cloud the garment thereof, and thick darkness a swaddlingband for it,

10 And brake up for it my decreed place, and set bars and doors,

11 And said, Hitherto shalt thou come, but no further: and here shall thy proud waves be stayed?"

God also told Job that He had reserved the ice and snow for a special time, a time that our militarists would call "J-Day." God put it this way:

Job 38
22 Hast thou entered into the treasures of the snow? or hast thou seen the treasures of the hail,
23 Which I have reserved against the time of trouble, against the day of battle and war?

It has long been suspected that there was in the snow some secret of nature which, when discovered, would reveal a new and unexpected source of power to be used in the last war, known as Armageddon. This could be. Snow and ice are produced by laws which seem to be the exception in nature. Heat is supposed to expand a material and cold to contract it. That is generally true. It is only partly true of water. Heat expands water into steam; but cold also expands water into ice and snow. You put antifreeze into your radiators in the winter because the freezing water would expand and burst the radiator. Snow is water, greatly expanded. This is contrary to the rule. Cold should contract water, not expand it. There is a secret of nature concealed in the snow and in the ice.

But "treasures of the snow" could mean large amounts stored up for use at a certain time. The fact that Job mentions hail rather than ice in this connection would seem to suggest that God is talking about a secret held in the snow and hail. It is doubtful that Job is using hail in the sense of great sheets of ice because he knew about ice and mentions it in:

Job 38
29 Out of whose womb came the ice? and the hoary frost of heaven, who hath gendered it?

Job mentions snow and hail separately. It may be they are to be used in two different ways. Much of the ice at the Arctic is the result of snow which, for years, has been falling on the earth and staying there to form ice, and building up to a height sometimes reaching 8,000 feet.

This may well be the first great sign of the approaching end of the age. It connects with more prophecy than anything that has happened to date and could bring the whole prophetic picture rushing down upon us.

It must be remembered that we are dealing with cycles of heat and cold. A series of cold winters may follow the warm ones. Then too, there are man-made conditions that affect climate such as the excessive use of coal or other products that would put impurities into the air, thus reducing the effect of the sun's rays. This would tend to produce extra cold in the winter. There are so many factors which enter into the changing climate that we cannot make short-term predictions.

The overall temperature summer and winter will coincide with Bible prophecy so that physical conditions on the earth will be exactly right to produce the conditions prophesied in the Bible.

Another Flood

If the long accumulated ice and snow should melt slowly, causing the ocean to rise slowly, and nothing else should happen in connection with it, that would hardly fulfill prophecy. The prophecies seem to indicate a sudden or flash flood. For instance:

Jeremiah 51
42 The sea is come up upon Babylon: she is covered with the multitude of the waves thereof.

43 Her cities are a desolation, a dry land, and a wilderness, a land wherein no man dwelleth, neither doth any son of man pass thereby.

The waters will not cover Babylon permanently. The land will dry up. Many other elements enter into the destruction of Babylon. The flood is the beginning of the end, but not the end of Babylon.

There are many prophecies in Isaiah, Jeremiah and Ezekiel concerning cities and nations that were not completely fulfilled, and even if there was somewhat of a fulfillment, it had no special significance. These prophecies all connect with the return of the Jews and the Day of the Lord. The solution lies in a fact that has not been completely comprehended. Circumstance will reveal it.

It is suggested first in Daniel's interpretation of Nebuchadnezzar's dream. The four world empires pictured in the image came and went exactly according to the prophecy. The gold had its day and disappeared. The silver, the brass and the iron followed in succession, till finally the Roman Empire divided into many countries represented by the toes of iron and clay.

Then a strange thing happened. The stone that was cut out without hand, which, according to Daniel, was the Kingdom of God, struck the image on its toes. When that happened, the entire image crumbled and the wind blew it away. Daniel is specific about it. He says the gold, the silver, the brass, the iron and clay, all turned to powder and the wind blew it away. But the empires represented by the gold, silver, brass and iron have long since passed into history. How, then, could they be destroyed at the coming of Christ?

There is one answer, which is borne out by many other prophecies. The image will stand again. Of course, those empires cannot be reconstituted exactly as they were in their glory, because the territory overlapped, or in some cases, was almost the same.

We sometimes speak of the revival of the Roman Empire, but the so-called revival is not confined to the Roman Empire. There is to be a revival of Bible lands. Palestine will be the "center of the earth." Worldwide wealth will flow out of Babylon. It all began there—it will also end there.

So we have thoughout prophecy a number of predictions which were never exactly fulfilled, and which seemed impossible of fulfillment because those places are gone, or are of no importance now. This will change —in fact, it is changing now. The world's attention will soon be centered on Bible lands. That is where the great changes will take place.

Babylon

There is nothing but sand now on the site of ancient Babylon. The rebuilding of that city will be one of the most sensational prophetic fulfillments. Our basic rule of interpretation is: If a prophecy never has been fulfilled, then it is to be fulfilled. The prophecies concerning Babylon were not fulfilled. Many of them are quoted in Revelation and applied to a future city and world religious system with its seat in Babylon. For instance, the following is said concerning a future city:

Revelation 18
2 Babylon is fallen, is fallen, and is become the habitation of devils, and the hold of every foul spirit, and a cage of every unclean and hateful bird.

This is taken directly from:

Isaiah 21
9 Babylon is fallen, is fallen; and all the graven

images of her gods he hath broken unto the ground.

Revelation 18

4 And I heard another voice from heaven, saying, Come out of her, my people, that ye be not partakers of her sins, and that ye receive not of her plagues.

5 For her sins have reached unto heaven, and God hath remembered her iniquities.

6 Reward her even as she rewarded you, double unto her and double according to her works: in the cup which she hath filled fill to her double.

7 How much she hath glorified herself, and lived deliciously, so much torment and sorrow give her: for she saith in her heart, I sit a queen, and am no widow, and shall see no sorrow.

8 Therefore shall her plagues come in one day, death, and mourning, and famine; and she shall be utterly burned with fire: for strong is the Lord God who judgeth her.

Isaiah 48

20 Go ye forth of Babylon, flee ye from the Chaldeans, with a voice of singing declare ye, tell this, utter it even to the end of the earth; say ye, The Lord hath redeemed his servant Jacob.

Jeremiah 50

39 Therefore the wild beasts of the desert with the wild beasts of the islands shall dwell there, and the owls shall dwell therein: and it shall be no more inhabited for ever; neither shall it be dwelt in from generation to generation.

Jeremiah 51

6 Flee out of the midst of Babylon, and deliver every man his soul: be not cut off in her iniquity; for this is the time of the Lord's vengeance; he will render unto her a recompence.

9 We would have healed Babylon, but she is not healed: forsake her, and let us go every one into

his own country: for her judgment reacheth unto heaven, and is lifted up even to the skies.

45 My people, go ye out of the midst of her, and deliver ye every man his soul from the fierce anger of the Lord.

Zechariah 2
7 Deliver thyself, O Zion, that dwellest with the daughter of Babylon.

Isaiah 13 could apply to nothing but the future Babylon. The time is stated as the day of the Lord, and the signs of that day are mentioned.

Isaiah 13
6 Howl ye; for the day of the Lord is at hand; it shall come as a destruction from the Almighty.

10 For the stars of heaven and the constellations thereof shall not give their light: the sun shall be darkened in his going forth, and the moon shall not cause her light to shine.

19 And Babylon, the glory of kingdoms, the beauty of the Chaldees' excellency, shall be as when God overthrew Sodom and Gomorrah.

None of the prophecies concerning the fall of Babylon were fulfilled. Babylon was never so destroyed. It is not noted for doleful creatures. These things are all future. Babylon must be rebuilt.

The prophecies concerning Babylon imply tremendous changes in that part of the world. Not the least of these changes involves religion. Today Babylon is a part of the Arab world. The Arabs are Mohammedan. The new city will not be Mohammedan, but the seat of a worldwide religion. It could include Mohammedanism, but Romanism is certainly involved. Babylon was the place of origin of all idolatrous religions. It was there that Satan tried to unite all such worship into one world religion. This would have given Satan almost complete and perpetual control of the world. Satan will almost accomplish this again at Babylon. After Babylon, the seat of Satan's religious activities was Pergamos, "where Satan's seat is" (Rev. 2:13); from there it went to Rome. From Rome it will return to Babylon; there it will forever be destroyed. The importance of Babylon may be realized from the amount of space given to it: two and a half chapters in Revelation—more than that given to any other subject—and many chapters in the Old Testament.

Jeremiah 51

41 How is Sheshach taken! and how is the praise of the whole earth surprised! how is Babylon become an astonishment among the nations!

42 The sea is come up upon Babylon: she is covered with the multitude of the waves thereof.

43 Her cities are a desolation, a dry land, and a wilderness, a land wherein no man dwelleth, neither doth any son of man pass thereby.

44 And I will punish Bel in Babylon, and I will bring forth out of his mouth that which he hath swallowed up: and the nations shall not flow together any more unto him: yea, the wall of Babylon shall fall.

Babylon is about 300 miles north of the Persian Gulf, on the Euphrates River. The flood will not come from the river, but from the sea. It is caused by a sudden rising of the sea. A tidal wave may also figure in the flash flood.

"Her cities are a desolation, a dry land" may refer to a time after the flood when Babylon is completely destroyed as Jeremiah goes on to say. It could also be applied to Babylon before the time of her restoration. Babylon is a dry land now. Then it would mean that a land as dry as Babylon and as far from the sea will be flooded from the sea, so high will the water come.

Tyre

Tyre was a great city in its day, but never was it anything like the prophets described it. The large amount of space given to the future of Tyre shows its importance in the empire of Antichrist. It will be his capital.

The Prince of Tyrus of Ezekiel 28:1-10 is not a type of Antichrist. He is Antichrist. The King of Tyrus of Ezekiel 28:11-19 is not a type of Satan. He is Satan.

Tyre will rival Babylon in splendor; in fact, its beauty is described in more detail.

Ezekiel 27

2 Now, thou son of man, take up a lamentation for Tyrus;

3 And say unto Tyrus, O thou that art situate at the entry of the sea, which art a merchant of the people for many isles, Thus saith the Lord God; O Tyrus, thou hast said, I am of perfect beauty.

4 Thy borders are in the midst of the seas, thy builders have perfected thy beauty.

5 They have made all thy ship boards of fir trees of Senir: they have taken cedars from Lebanon to make masts for thee.

6 Of the oaks of Bashan have they made thine oars; the company of the Ashurites have made thy benches of ivory, brought out of the isles of Chittim.

7 Fine linen with broidered work from Egypt was that which thou spreadest forth to be thy sail; blue and purple from the isles of Elishah was that which covered thee.

27 Thy riches, and thy fairs, thy merchandise, thy mariners, and thy pilots, thy calkers, and the

occupiers of thy merchandise, and all thy men of war, that are in thee, and in all thy company which is in the midst of thee, shall fall into the midst of the seas in the day of thy ruin.

It will be interesting to watch the rebuilding of Tyre because it will follow exactly the Bible blueprint. Tyre is on the Mediterranean Sea, an island or point off the coast of Lebanon, not very far north of Palestine. It will be destroyed by the coming flood.

Ezekiel 27
34 In the time when thou shalt be broken by the seas in the depths of the waters thy merchandise and all thy company in the midst of thee shall fall.

Jeremiah, when recording the flood, adds an important detail. He tells where the flood waters come from.

Jeremiah 47
2 Thus saith the Lord; Behold, waters rise up out of the north, and shall be an overflowing flood, and shall overflow the land, and all that is therein; the city, and them that dwell therein: then the men shall cry, and all the inhabitants of the land shall howl.

The waters that cause this prophesied flash flood will come from the north according to Jeremiah.

Waters are sometimes used as symbols of peoples or armies, in symbolical portions of scripture, as in:

Revelation 17
15 And he saith unto me, The waters which thou sawest, where the whore sitteth, are peoples, and multitudes, and nations, and tongues.

In the 16th chapter of Revelation there is a mention of the water of the river Euphrates.

Revelation 16
12 And the sixth angel poured out his vial upon

the great river Euphrates; and the water thereof was dried up, that the way of the kings of the east might be prepared.

This could, in a sense, be symbolical of the overthrow of the country that will, in that day, be the successor to the Babylonian Empire, but that would have to be a secondary interpretation. This is not water in the abstract, but a definite river. It is named. Here the water of the Euphrates is meant.

Always, in the absence of apparent symbolical intent, the literal interpretation must be first applied.

This flood on the coastal lands of the Mediterranean is to come from the north. The waters are to rise up in the north and come down.

There seems to be a difference in the reports coming from the South Pole and the North Pole. The South Pole region is mostly land. A great continent is there covered with ice. The North Pole is water. Land areas of Canada, Greenland, Russia, and Alaska reach into the icecap, but aside from that the icecap is on water.

Reports from the south so far indicate that the ocean is rising as a result of the melting ice.

Reports from the north are to the effect that the land is rising as the weight of ice and snow is lessened. This may not continue through the whole process. The crust of the earth, compressed so long, could hold its shape for the most part until a certain time, then let go all at once.

The ocean may rise gradually to a certain extent, but the time is coming when a great flood wave will sweep down from the north. How many countries will suffer a flood we do not know. Prophecy mentions only those that are in Bible lands. Amos, however, suggests that the flood will be somewhat universal.

Amos 9
6 He that calleth for the waters of the sea, and

poureth them out upon the face of the earth: The Lord is his name.

This is very vivid language. In a very peculiar sense, this water belongs to God. He put it in the heavens. He sent it down upon the earth when men became so wicked there was no hope for them. He set bars and gates of ice to hold it in place until a certain time when He will call for it and pour it out upon the face of the earth. This flood will not be universal as was the flood of Noah's day. God never again will destroy all mankind from the face of the earth. It is the coastal lands that are mostly affected, but the whole world would suffer from such a flood.

The statements of scientists that most nearly conform to the prophecy are those relating to the rise of the crust of the earth when the weight is released. This phenomenon is not apparent at the South Pole, but it is in the north. The lowering of the level of Hudson Bay and the rising of the Great Lakes would seem to imply some such action.

Of course, the big, sudden rise has not yet come, and will not come until a certain amount of ice has melted; then we can expect a sudden upheaval over a great area.

This flood is set for some time in the future, as we shall see when we examine the prophecies that indicate the time—the time, that is, in reference to other prophetic events.

The first sign has come. The speed with which the ice is melting is of great concern right now. That seems to have been a matter for alarm to those men who went south for a firsthand investigation.

Telegrams and radio messages have to be brief and every word is packed with meaning. One of the big points emphasized in the messages from the South Pole was the fast rate of melting. "Explanation definitely to be sought in melting processes of Antarctic ice."

The first message was sent, apparently, soon after arrival. The icecap itself had not been examined. The conclusion was drawn from the amount of water flooding the lowlands.

Added to this is another fact which connects with the finding of Professor Huntington of Yale some years ago, that the rise of four degrees in the world's temperature would melt all the ice at the poles.

The message from the South Pole Expedition ended with the startling statement: "Temperature in the Central Ice District four degrees higher than two years ago."

Again we have speed emphasized. Only two years— four degrees in two years! That is enough to start the process. That is, in fact, the exact amount that is needed to start the process, as determined by scientists years ago; from now on, the process will be automatic. All the ice will eventually melt. The only question now is: How fast? How near are we to the end of the age?

Here we have the most important sign that could be imagined, because it is one that we can watch. The weather is something that everybody can understand. It brings into purview the entire prophetic picture. It connects with a large segment of prophecy which must now be studied.

For instance, we have the specific prophecy that a sudden flood will come from the north. Why not the south, or from both directions at once?

In the north the great icecap is mostly on water. There is no great body of land at the North Pole, but great land areas of both hemispheres extend into the ice area. As the ice melts, the crust of the earth rises and the water runs toward the south, raising the level of the lakes and even the ocean.

The *Saturday Evening Post* of July 17, 1954, has

a story on the U.S. Geological Survey by Harold H. Martin which makes this significant statement:

> The West Coast right now is rising slowly and tilting toward the East, and the East Coast, south of New York, is slowly sinking. Nobody knows why. North of New York the land is rising, but there is a reason for that. The earth that was pressed down under the great weight of the glaciers is slowly regaining its original shape.

Suddenly, something will happen in the north that will cause a great wave of water to sweep down and flood coastal lands.

In the winter of 1976-1977 the United States experienced unusually cold weather. At the same time, Alaska had an unusually warm winter. There were times when the temperature of Anchorage was higher than that of Atlanta, Georgia. The weather in Alaska is more significant than the weather farther south because it presages a warmer climate throughout the world.

Earthquakes

Habakkuk also mentions this sudden flood; but Habakkuk is a poet, and he uses the imagery of a poet.

Habakkuk 3
10 The mountains saw thee, and they trembled: the overflowing of the water passed by: the deep uttered his voice, and lifted up his hands on high.

If the ice melted slowly, a little each year, it would not cause a sudden flood, but a gradual rise of the ocean level. However, the earth's crust is not absolutely solid. It contains water, gas, oil and many cracks. It is, in effect, spongy. The tremendous weight of the surplus water at the poles has compressed the crust of the earth; it is rising slightly as the ice melts, but it could someday suddenly spring up into its original form causing a tremendous flood. It is something like this that is indicated in many prophecies.

This sudden shift in the weight of the earth will have other results. It is quite certain that the water there froze suddenly. The reason the poles are cold is that the earth is inclined 23 1/2 degrees to the plane of its orbit. The earth does not present a solid front to the sun, but is tipped so that for six months the North Pole is dark because it is tipped away from the sun. The same is true of the South Pole but in opposite season. If this is the cause of the cold, and if the cold came suddenly, then the earth must have tipped suddenly.

Following this same logic, if the water should suddenly leave the poles and run down over the earth, it could cause another tipping, a sudden movement in the opposite direction.

In this connection Mr. Baxter almost quotes Scripture, possibly without realizing it. In answer to his question: "Why have the waters of the Great Lakes gone crazy?" he quotes Dr. Richard F. Flint of Yale University who thinks that the entire northern portion of our continent is tilting upwards. During the ice age the billions of tons of ice in the Arctic depressed the crust of the earth. As the heat zone of the earth moves northward, the ice melts and conditions are reversed. If this continues, the lakes will rise to a place where whole new rivers will come into existence flowing south into the Ohio and Mississippi valleys.

An English scientist, Sir Cyril Fox, in a book called *Water* says:

> With the withdrawal of the ice sheets and the consequent unloading, the crust will rise. This has happened in North America in the region of the Great

Lakes, and the slow uplift appears to be still in progress and affects the drainage of the region. The Ottawa River, for example, once drained the lakes, which now discharge into the St. Lawrence River. In the future, if the land continues to rise, the Mississippi will draw its water from Lake Superior, while its tributaries, the Illinois and Ohio, will tap the other lakes, Michigan and Erie.

Then Mr. Baxter quotes a hydrographer, H. Auchinoloss Brown, who supports this theory that the poles are getting lighter and our part of the earth is getting heavier. Mr. Brown says that in about every 8,000 years the ice at the pole gets so heavy that first it causes the earth to wobble on its axis and finally to overturn. Then Mr. Baxter comments that the earth is now very wobbly and is getting ready to "flop over."

This is exactly what Isaiah predicted of the Day of the Lord.

Isaiah 24

18 The foundations of the earth do shake.

19 The earth is utterly broken down, the earth is clean dissolved, the earth is moved exceedingly.

20 The earth shall reel to and fro like a drunkard. . . .

Mr. Baxter says "wobble." Isaiah says "reel." There is no difference.

Earthquakes are a feature of the last days of this age. They begin with the tribulation period and continue through to the return of Christ, when the final big one comes, the one that moves the entire earth.

Revelation 16

18 And there were voices, and thunders, and lightnings; and there was a great earthquake, such as was not since men were upon the earth, so mighty an earthquake, and so great.

19 And the great city was divided into three parts, and the cities of the nations fell: and great Babylon came in remembrance before God, to give unto her the cup of the wine of the fierceness of his wrath.

20 And every island fled away, and the mountains were not found.

Matthew 24

7 For nation shall rise against nation, and kingdom against kingdom: and there shall be famines, and pestilences, and earthquakes, in divers places.

This marks the beginning of the tribulation, as Jesus says in:

Matthew 24

8 All these are the beginning of sorrows.

This is described more fully in

Revelation 6

12 And I beheld when he had opened the sixth seal, and, lo, there was a great earthquake; and the sun became black as sackcloth of hair, and the moon became as blood;

13 And the stars of heaven fell unto the earth, even as a fig tree casteth her untimely figs, when she is shaken of a mighty wind.

14 And the heaven departed as a scroll when it is rolled together; and every mountain and island were moved out of their places.

15 And the kings of the earth, and the great men, and the rich men, and the chief captains, and the mighty men, and every bondman, and every free man, hid themselves in the dens and in the rocks of the mountains;

16 And said to the mountains and rocks, Fall on us, and hide us from the face of him that sitteth on the throne, and from the wrath of the Lamb:

17 For the great day of his wrath is come; and who shall be able to stand?

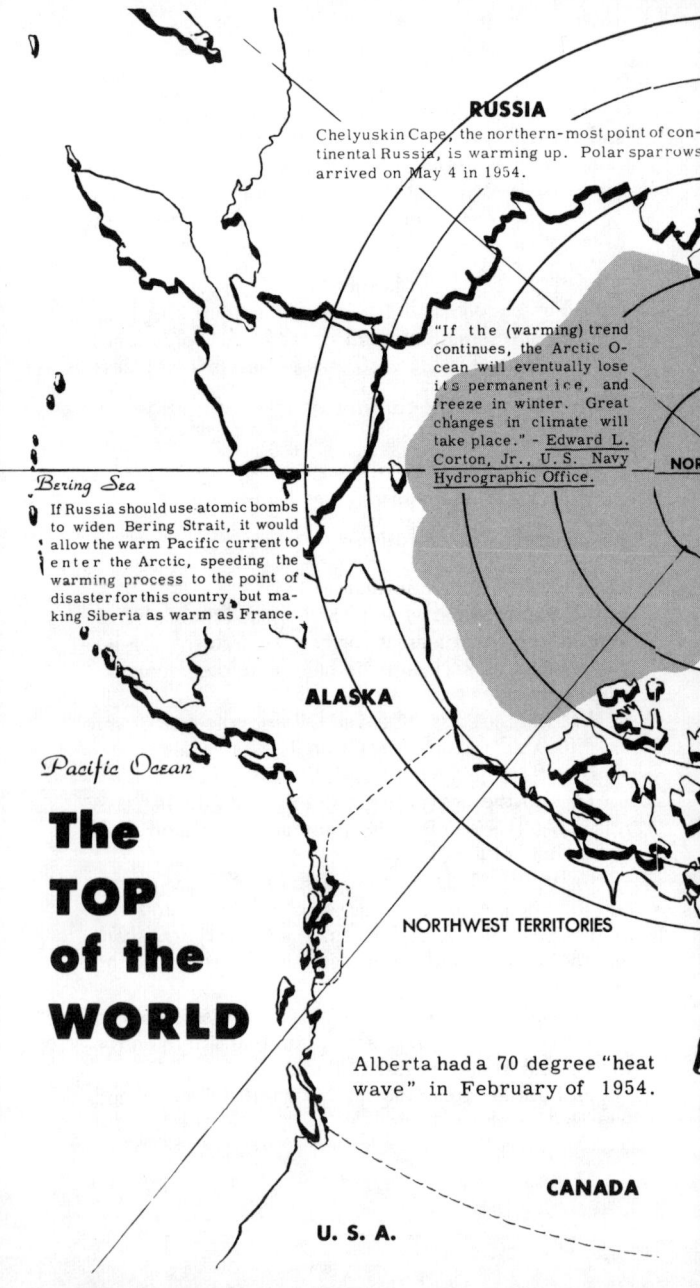

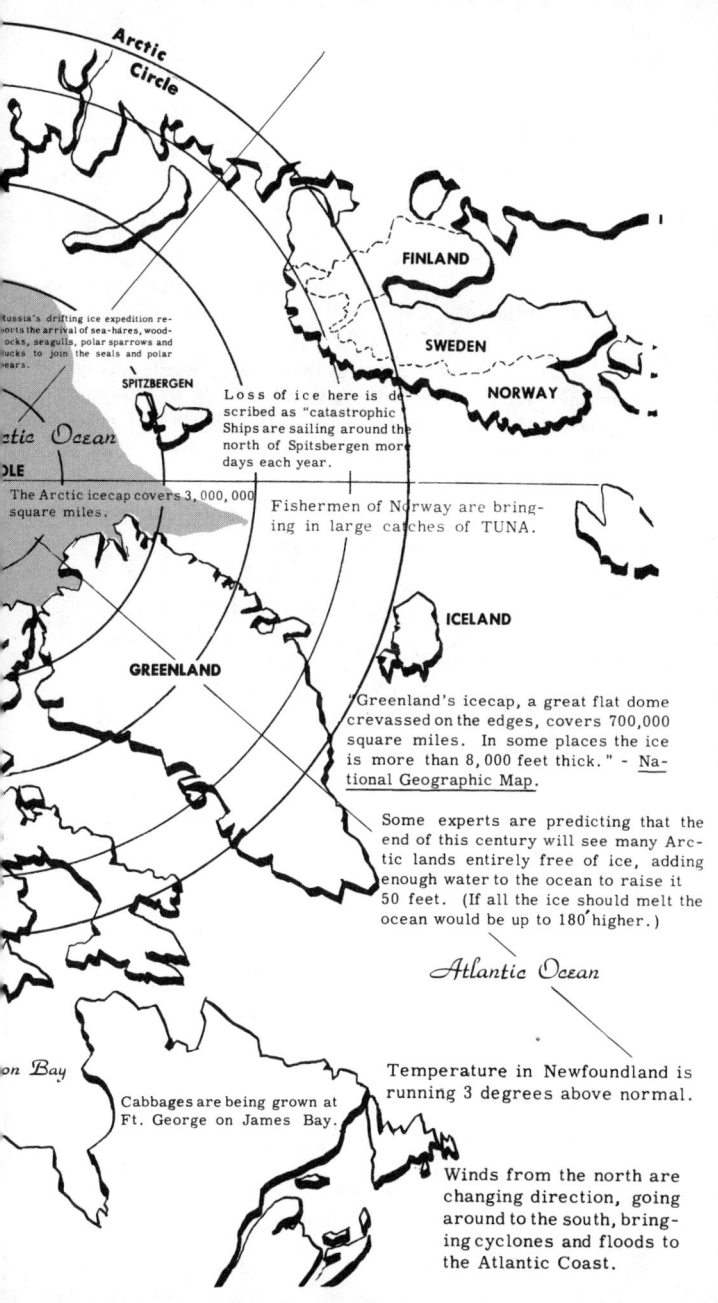

These earthquakes follow all through the "Day of the Lord" till the coming of Christ. They are mentioned from time to time throughout Revelation.

Revelation 8

5 And the angel took the censer, and filled it with fire of the altar, and cast it into the earth: and there were voices, and thunderings, and lightnings, and an earthquake.

Revelation 11

13 And the same hour was there a great earthquake, and the tenth part of the city fell, and in the earthquake were slain of men seven thousand: and the remnant were affrighted, and gave glory to the God of heaven.

It is to this series of earthquakes that Isaiah refers in the second chapter when he says:

Isaiah 2

20 In that day a man shall cast his idols of silver and his idols of gold, which they made each one for himself to worship, to the moles and to the bats;

21 To go into the clefts of the rocks, and into the tops of the ragged rocks, for fear of the Lord, and for the glory of his majesty, when he ariseth to shake terribly the earth.

These earthquakes could well be caused by the "wobbling" of the earth when the weight begins to shift from the north to the temperate zones. The result of the rising crust of the earth in the north is already noticed in the level of the ocean and the fluctuation of the level of the Great Lakes. But only a very small portion of the ice has melted. It is true the icecap is receding, but only by a very small percentage. Yet that small amount can have far-reaching effects on the water, the climate, the rainfall and the winds.

If something like half of the ice should melt over a period of time, the result would be almost inconceivable. Much less than that would frighten the world and cause a movement of peoples, the like of which this world has never seen.

It is no wonder that scientists are saying that a rise of only two degrees in the world's temperature would have disastrous effects on mankind. Such a change in the earth's crust as this condition would bring would certainly cause unexpected earthquakes in many new places.

As an example of what is happening underground, I read a newspaper account of a strange thing that happened in a southern state. It was unusually dry, and new, supposedly deeper, wells had to be dug. They got their heavy machinery together for the purpose of digging a deep well, but in a short time they had a gusher of water. The reporter explained that the pressure of the extra water in the Great Lakes had forced a new stream to flow through the crevices of the earth. It had reached to the southern states.

Not only is the temperature above the earth changing, but the earth underneath is undergoing a change. This must be added to all the other signs.

The Coming Flood—When?

Newsweek has suggested that a flood could be caused by the breaking up of the Greenland ice, and other icecaps, by atomic explosions.

Atomic explosions are mere firecrackers, playthings, as compared to the powers of nature that only God controls. When one of the great cyclones was raging past New York City, a New York newspaper reported a scientist as saying that for man to reproduce the force displayed in that cyclone he would have to set off six atomic bombs a minute.

It so happens that the time of this particular flood

can be determined in reference to other prophecies. One of the Old Testament prophets puts this flood in a setting which connects with Revelation, and therefore its time may be determined. Revelation gives us a sequence of events, for there the events are numbered. We will, therefore, explore this prophecy at great length. It points to the sixth chapter of Revelation, and there we find the events that will satisfy the conditions laid down by *Newsweek* for the breaking up of that icecap. See Revelation 6:12-17 quoted in the previous section, "Earthquakes."

These falling stars and earthquakes will be enough to chop up all the ice on Greenland and dump it into the surrounding warm water. This may be the reason Jeremiah said the flood waters will come "out of the north."

Wherever a Bible prophecy is examined the first question which comes to mind is, When? It is not merely a matter of curiosity; it is one of the first points to be considered in the process of interpretation. Rightly dividing the Word of Truth is, in part at least, putting it in its proper sequence.

The importance of this question will be at once recognized when we consider the seven last plagues of Revelation, the trumpets and vials. They lead directly to the return of Christ in glory. The time of these events is, therefore, firmly established.

The first four are the ones that directly concern us in connection with the changing climate, because there the prevailing factor is heat. Fire from the heaven strikes the earth, the sea, the rivers, and the sky—all producing extreme heat. All the green grass is burned up and one-third of the trees, and men blaspheme God because of the heat. There would not be much icecap left after that; although even that heat, for so short a time, would probably not melt all that ice.

The big question is: Will the water that causes the flood, mentioned in so many prophecies, come from the north before or after the first four plagues of Revelation?

The prophecies of a flood all apply to a general time which could be somewhat previous to those final events, and there is no mention of a flood after the plagues, except in:

Daniel 9
26 And the end thereof shall be with a flood.

This flood of Daniel's has another cause that is also the subject of prophecy. It concerns only Jerusalem which is too high to be flooded from the sea. It is caused by a river gushing forth out of the ground and flowing in two directions, as a result of the final and greatest earthquake.

Zechariah 14
8 And it shall be in that day, that living waters shall go out from Jerusalem; half of them toward the former sea, and half of them toward the hinder sea: in summer and in winter shall it be.

Ezekiel 47
1 Afterward he brought me again unto the door of the house; and, behold, waters issued out from under the threshold of the house eastward: for the forefront of the house stood toward the east, and the waters came down from under from the right side of the house, at the south side of the altar.

2 Then brought he me out of the way of the gate northward, and led me about the way without unto the utter gate by the way that looketh eastward; and, behold, there ran out waters on the right side.

3 And when the man that had the line in his hand went forth eastward, he measured a thousand cubits, and he brought me through the waters; the waters were to the ancles.

4 Again he measured a thousand, and brought me through the waters; the waters were to the knees. Again he measured a thousand, and brought me through; the waters were to the loins.

5 Afterward he measured a thousand; and it was a river that I could not pass over: for the waters were risen, waters to swim in, a river that could not be passed over.

The terrific heat of the last days before the return of Christ, during 3 1/2 years of which there will be no rain, would do one of two things:

(1) If the polar ice were still there, it would melt most of it.

(2) If the polar ice were already melted, it would evaporate the water pulling it into the sky, thus removing it from the earth and restoring it to its original position above the firmament.

The question, therefore, is: Will the icecap be melted before or during the great heat wave from heaven?

This brings us to the question: When will the prophesied flood come?

The prophecies quoted so far all apply to a general time previous to the final events. There is one prophecy, however, that seems to pinpoint the time, but it requires a little explanation.

Habakkuk 3
10 The mountains saw thee, and they trembled: the overflowing of the water passed by: the deep uttered his voice, and lifted up his hands on high.

The third chapter of Habakkuk is parallel to the sixth chapter of Revelation. Revelation has been so badly treated by its friends that I refer to it only if I have to. In this instance it is a chapter that has been especially misconstrued. Some explanation will be necessary.

The scene of the sixth chapter of Revelation is in heaven around the throne. The time is immediately after the resurrection. On earth the tribulation has begun.

The saints are in heaven. They are gathered around the throne, ready for the action which will follow the breaking of the seals. The saints are not all in one group, but are divided into companies preparatory to the work that is to be done.

I Corinthians 6
2 Do ye not know that the saints shall judge the world? . . .

Psalm 149
5 Let the saints be joyful in glory: let them sing aloud upon their beds.

6 Let the high praises of God be in their mouth, and a two-edged sword in their hand;

7 To execute vengeance upon the heathen [nations], and punishments upon the people;

8 To bind their kings with chains, and their nobles with fetters of iron;

9 To execute upon them the judgment written: this honour have all his saints. Praise ye the Lord.

The groups are called by new names: elders, living ones (erroneously called beasts in the Authorized Version), horsemen, and angels.

There is a division of work. We will be made rulers over many things according to our faithfulness over few things. The elders, horsemen, and others, all redeemed from the earth, "execute the judgments written" in the seven-sealed book that is about to be opened.

The Lamb breaks a seal, the living one gives the order, the horseman carries it out. The particular work to be done is to preach the gospel to every kindred, tongue, people and nation under the pressure of judgments from heaven. It is judgment mixed with grace.

Three of the horsemen have to do with wrath; one

has charge of the Word, the gospel. The results of this work are told in the seventh chapter of Revelation: 144,000 Israelites are saved together with a multitude of people from every nation.

It is during this time that many prophecies will come to a head. It is a time of tremendous agitation both from heaven and from Antichrist.

The sixth chapter of Revelation is one of the most important chapters in prophecy, and it is tragic that it has been so badly treated by its friends that it has put a cloud over many other prophetic passages.

A large portion deals with the time between the resurrection and the second coming of Christ. This part of Revelation is in two distinct stories. First, there is the story of what happens in heaven during that time; and second, the story of what happens on earth during that time.

In the first story, with which we are now dealing, the scene is in heaven. Of course, the earth is in view at times because heaven is dealing with the earth; but the whole story is told from the standpoint of heaven, as one in heaven looking down to the earth. This has confused many interpreters because it is the first time a thing like this has happened in the Bible. It is the first time we have been given a record of heavenly and earthly activities written by someone in heaven looking down upon the earth.

We have, in the Old Testament, a number of instances when heavenly things have been seen—even God upon His throne; but it is always from the standpoint of someone on the earth looking up or seeing a vision, and the story is written by a seer right here on the earth.

Now, for the first time, a reporter has been caught up in spirit into heaven and has experienced the processes that will take place in heaven after the resurrection. He writes this from the heavenly viewpoint. The elders, the living ones, the horsemen, and the angels are all heavenly beings, or, at least beings in heaven, although they may have come from the earth by way of resurrection or translation. In fact, in one place they say they are redeemed from every tongue, people and nation. They are now in heaven. The resurrection has taken place; they have their new immortal bodies. They are preparing to carry out the remainder of the program of redemption which was begun on the earth, and in which they had a part. They are now going to finish the task. There is actually no difference in the work that is being done. It is the consummation of the redemptive program of the saints, with the exception that they now hold the position of power that Satan once had. They have actually changed places with Satan who is the prince of the power of the air.

Satan is going to be cast out of his high places down to the earth, at the resurrection, at the same time the saints will be caught up into heaven and will continue to operate from that vantage point.

This part of Revelation is the story of the saints in heaven. It tells what will happen among the saints after the resurrection; therefore, we should never treat these groups as symbolic of something on the earth. Heavenly things are never symbols. They are literal, but they are not of the earth. The living ones, the elders, the horsemen, and the angels (messengers) are merely names of the groups into which the saints are assembled for the purpose at hand, namely, the redemption of the earth.

They are all heavenly beings, having been redeemed from the earth, not as symbols of something else. The things they do must be treated as literally true; but we must understand that we are dealing with heavenly things for which there are no earthly words. John had to use words of this world to express things and thoughts which have no exact counterpart.

To treat these words in a symbolic sense and apply them to earthly things creates a confusion which makes it almost impossible to connect these great prophecies with the other prophecies of the Bible which are certainly parallel.

Let us get this in mind. The resurrection has just taken place. The saints have been translated into heaven. Satan is reigning in person on this earth in the body of Antichrist. He is planning to destroy the world. He has great wrath because he knows he has but a short time. There will be a relentless persecution, even unto death, of all those who confess Christ. The war in heaven has been transferred to the earth.

This war is carried on by the saints themselves with Christ leading them as He opens the seals of the book. Let us follow the course of events as John saw it.

Revelation 6

1 And I saw when the Lamb opened one of the seals, and I heard, as it were the noise of thunder, one of the four beasts saying, Come and see.

Two corrections should be made in the translation of this verse. The word for beasts should be read "living ones." The Revised Version has living creatures. The emphasis is on the word living; they are those who once lived on the earth and were subject to death, but now have everlasting life. They are living ones.

The command "come and see" is a questionable translation. The Revised Version reads simply "come." The words "and see" are in some of the ancient manuscripts, but the command is not to John. He did not have to be told to pay attention. The command is to the horseman. He is told to come (or go), and he goes forth conquering.

So, a good rendering would be: "And I saw when the Lamb opened one of the seals, and I heard, as it were, the noise of thunder, one of the living ones saying, "Go."

Revelation 6
2 And I saw, and behold a white horse: and he that sat on him had a bow; and a crown was given unto him: and he went forth conquering, and to conquer.

Please do not call the first horseman "Antichrist." That is an insult. You yourselves may be among the number that are represented by this rider on the white horse who comes out from heaven in response to the command of the living one and as a result of the breaking of a seal by the Lamb.

We will hear about Antichrist when we get to the second section of this Revelation story which deals with the events as they occur on the earth. It has been argued that Antichrist is a deceiver and that he is pictured here in his assumed character instead of his real character, thus accounting for the white horse, the crown, the bow, and the victory.

Such exegesis would put a question mark after every Bible description and make consistent interpretation almost impossible. There is no evidence that Antichrist will be a messiah or that the Jews will ever receive him as such. It is true he will confirm the covenant with many. It is assumed that the many referred to are Jews; but treaties are not made by a ruler with his own nation. The President, for instance, may make a treaty with France, but he could not make a treaty with the United States, of which he is president. Rulers do not make treaties with their own nations; they make them with foreign countries. Therefore, the very fact that he will confirm the covenant with the Jews is evidence that he is a foreigner and considered a foreign ruler.

He is Antichrist, not because he imitates Christ, but because he opposes Christ. The world will worship him, not because they think he is Christ, but because of his military might.

Revelation 13
4 They worshipped the beast, saying, Who is like unto the beast? who is able to make war with him?

The horsemen ride variously colored horses. The colors do not represent the nature of the rider, but the nature of the work to be done. It is the horse, not the rider, that is colored. White connects with righteousness. In Revelation, white is used in reference to Christ, the saints, and the throne of God. It is never used of Antichrist.

The result accomplished by this horseman is represented by white and it has something to do with righteousness. In this day of the consummation of redemption four things must be done.

(1) Everyone must hear the gospel and have a chance to repent.

Matthew 24
14 And this gospel of the kingdom shall be preached in all the world for a witness unto all nations; and then shall the end come.

(2) The nations must be judged and purged.

Revelation 14
19 And the angel thrust in his sickle into the earth, and gathered the vine of the earth, and cast it into the great winepress of the wrath of God.

(3) That which cannot be redeemed must be destroyed.

Revelation 18

21 And a mighty angel took up a stone like a great millstone, and cast it into the sea, saying, Thus with violence shall that great city Babylon be thrown down, and shall be found no more at all.

(4) There must be a reconstruction to make all things new.

Revelation 21

5 And he that sat upon the throne said, Behold, I make all things new.

It should be understood that the terrible things coming upon the earth during those days are not the results of the workings of nature, neither are they brought about by the inventions of men. They are judgments sent directly from heaven upon the earth, and they are all for a purpose. The first ones, mentioned in this chapter, have a specific purpose connected with salvation. They accompany the preaching of the gospel to every kindred, tongue, people and nation. The people on the earth recognize these things as coming from heaven. That is probably one of the reasons why so great a multitude is saved, a multitude which no man could number.

Revelation 7

9 After this I beheld, and, lo, a great multitude, which no man could number, of all nations, and kindreds, and people, and tongues, stood before the throne, and before the Lamb, clothed with white robes, and palms in their hands.

These four horsemen, sent out from heaven to operate in the earth, cause the people of the earth to recognize the fact that they are dealing with God.

Revelation 6

15 And the kings of the earth, and the great men,

and the rich men, and the chief captains, and the mighty men, and every bondman, and every free man, hid themselves in the dens and in the rocks of the mountains;

16 And said to the mountains and rocks, Fall on us, and hide us from the face of him that sitteth on the throne, and from the wrath of the Lamb:

17 For the great day of his wrath is come; and who shall be able to stand?

This rider on the white horse also carried a bow, which is the Word of God.

Habakkuk 3

8 Was the Lord displeased against the rivers? was thine anger against the rivers? was thy wrath against the sea, that thou didst ride upon thine horses and thy chariots of salvation?

9 Thy bow was made quite naked, according to the oaths of the tribes, even thy word. Selah. Thou didst cleave the earth with rivers.

He also wore a crown. Antichrist also has a crown, but that word for crown is a different word entirely. Here the word used refers to the crowns of the saints.

Revelation 3

11 Behold, I come quickly: hold that fast which thou hast, that no man take thy crown.

He went forth "conquering and to conquer"; that is, to have the final victory. This word is found in only one other place in the New Testament:

Romans 8

37 Nay, in all these things we are more than conquerors through him that loved us.

The other three horsemen have been said to represent war, famine, and pestilence. The second horseman takes peace from the earth. That is when "nation shall rise against nation, and kingdom against kingdom."

If peace is taken from the earth, there would, of course, be wars, but much more than war is involved. There is strife among all peoples; capital and labor, city and farm; a man's foes shall be found even in his own household.

The third horseman has been said to represent famine or to bring famine to the earth. But that is not exactly what it says. Actually he is sent to prevent the world from starving when the famine comes. He is a sort of food administrator. The famine would be a natural result of peace being taken from the earth.

These horsemen operate all at once so that at the same time that wars, famines, and pestilences strike the earth, the gospel is preached from heaven to all nations. How this preaching appears to people on the earth may be read in:

Revelation 14
6 And I saw another angel [messenger] fly in the midst of heaven, having the everlasting gospel to preach unto them that dwell on the earth, and to every nation, and kindred, and tongue, and people.

Jesus mentioned these same things in connection with the tribulation which follows the resurrection when He said:

Matthew 24
7 For nation shall rise against nation, and kingdom against kingdom: and there shall be famines, and pestilences, and earthquakes, in divers places.

8 All these are the beginning of sorrows.

14 And this gospel of the kingdom shall be preached in all the world for a witness unto all nations; and then shall the end [end of the age] come.

Here we have a mixture of wrath and grace—wrath whose purpose is salvation. Here we have a revival in connection with the judgments of God. Notice that there are four features; three of them have reference to wrath and one has reference to grace or salvation.

Chapter 3 of Habakkuk

Now let us look at the third chapter of Habakkuk, which mentions the coming flood.

This is poetry and must be read as poetry. Habakkuk does not say crudely that the ocean will rise with a roar and threaten to engulf even the mountains. Rather, he says:

> Habakkuk 3
> 10 The mountains saw thee, and they trembled: the overflowing of the water passed by: the deep uttered his voice, and lifted up his hands on high.

It is called a prayer, although there is only one formal prayer in the poem.

> Habakkuk 3
> 2 O Lord, I have heard thy speech, and was afraid: O Lord, revive thy work in the midst of the years, in the midst of the years make known; in wrath remember mercy.

The rest of the prayer is a development of this one petition, that "in the midst of the years"—that is, in the last days when the consummation of redemption is about to be accomplished and God's wrath is about to be poured out upon the earth—God would first remember to accompany the wrath with mercy and grace. How this is to be accomplished is revealed in the prayer. It corresponds exactly with that which we read in Revelation and in the Olivet Discourse.

> Habakkuk 3
> 3 God came from Teman, and the Holy One from mount Paran. Selah. His glory covered the heavens, and the earth was full of his praise.

This is a reference to, if not a quotation from,

Deuteronomy 33
2 And he said, The Lord came from Sinai, and rose up from Seir unto them; he shined forth from mount Paran, and he came with ten thousands of saints: from his right hand went a fiery law for them.

"As he then came in glory to make a covenant with his people, so will he appear again in majesty to deliver them from the power of evil and to execute judgment. The prophet takes his stand in time preceding the action of the verb, and hence uses the future tense thus showing that he is prophesying of a great event to come symbolized by these earlier manifestations."—Pulpit Commentary.

" 'His glory covered the heavens.' His majestic brightness spread over the heavens, dimming the gleam of the sun and stars, and his boundless majesty fills the highest heavens and glorifies all its inhabitants."—Pulpit Commentary.

Matthew 13
43 Then shall the righteous shine forth as the sun in the kingdom of their Father.

This preaching of the gospel from heaven by the saints is going to be a glorious and spectacular affair.

Habakkuk 3
4 And his brightness was as the light; he had horns coming out of his hand: and there was the hiding of his power.

Rays of light, like horns, shone forth from His hand. This kind of simile is common in ancient poetry. "There was the hiding of his power." God hid himself in this light. It was the hiding place of His majesty. He clothes himself with light as with a garment. The world can see the brilliance; it cannot see God.

Habakkuk 3

5 Before him went the pestilence, and burning coals went forth at his feet.

This is the day of God's power. Of course, God always has power. Jesus said:

Matthew 28

18 All power is given unto me in heaven and in earth.

But to have power and to use power are two different things. God is long-suffering, not willing that any should perish, but the day of the Lord will come.

"Burning coals went forth at his feet." Habakkuk is not talking about the atom bomb or any man-made weapon; nor is he talking particularly about the forces of nature; but rather special judgments and wrath proceeding from the throne of God and administered by God's agents. They represent to the people on the earth the wrath and power of God. Everyone on earth recognizes this fact, and they cry to the mountains to shield them from the wrath of him that sits on the throne.

Habakkuk 3

6 He stood, and measured the earth: he beheld, and drove asunder the nations; and the everlasting mountains were scattered, the perpetual hills did bow: his ways are everlasting.

Habakkuk, in vision, sees God as He takes His stand and surveys the earth, which He is about to visit in judgment. As His glory filled the heavens, so now He, with His presence paces the earth, measuring it with His foot. This is an overall poetic statement, a summary of the whole process of redemption which is about to start and which will not stop until the kingdoms of this world have all become the kingdoms of our Lord.

Although the whole process is in view, Habakkuk

is given the details of only a portion, the first few years during which, as Habakkuk says in his opening prayer, mercy accompanies wrath.

"He drove asunder the nations." This prophecy is expanded in Revelation where the judgments of God are sent upon the nations—first, by taking peace from the earth, when nation shall rise against nation and kingdom against kingdom; second, by earthquakes, falling stars and fiery judgments; third, by the plagues that are sent directly upon the kingdom of the beast; and in the end, by the great battle of Armageddon.

"The everlasting mountains were scattered." This seems like a simple statement, yet in it is packed a volume of truth that science, today, is only beginning to spell out. Geologists are beginning to put together the history of the earth during the past few billion years.

Everything now points to the fact that the earth is several billion years old. Tremendous things have happened in the past ages before man, resulting in the coal fields, the oil wells, the diamond mines and many other features that are only now beginning to be understood. Scientists have divided the past into eras of millions of years duration, and they have given names to these long eras.

The oldest era is called the Archaen; then follows the Algonkian. These run back into billions of years. There are various ways of determining the age of the earth. They do not all agree as to the exact number of years, but they all indicate the earth has been here a very long time and many great and sometimes sudden changes have taken place. The Genesis account is one of these changes. It is amazing how closely the known facts, as they come out, correspond to Bible statements. That is especially illustrated in the results of climate change.

It is quite evident that there were forms of life on the earth before the chaos referred to in the second verse of Genesis.

Genesis 1
2 And the earth was without form, and void; and darkness was upon the face of the deep.

This life began in the era known as the Paleozoic. This was a time of mild climate from pole to pole and quiet as far as physical disturbances are concerned. It lasted for millions of years.

Then there came a time of worldwide revolution. Revolution is the name given by geologists to a time of great physical disturbance, such as the earth being without form and void, mentioned in Genesis. It does not have to be as great a catastrophe as that to be termed revolution. Ever since man has been on the earth we have lived in a time of revolution: earthquakes, volcanoes, storms, glaciers, freezing weather, tidal waves, floods, etc.

> It will be news to many people that man, during his geologically brief existence on earth, has never known a "normal" climate. We are now at the tail end of an ice age and living in a period of crustal and climate violence as great as any the earth has known. This is why we have to think so much about the weather. Such periods of revolution have occurred briefly several times in the history of the earth. Between them have been far longer periods of crustal peace and a genial climatic uniformity—the "normal" times of the geologist.—Yearbook of Agriculture, 1941.

The Mesozoic era is followed by the Cenozoic. The Cenozoic, in turn, is divided into periods called Tertiary and Quaternary. The Quaternary is divided into epochs called Pleistocene and Recent. The Recent includes the whole history of man.

There is a direct connection between mountains and climate. The normal condition of the earth is a mild, genial climate from pole to pole. That has been the condition on the earth for most of the millions of years of its past; only rarely does there come a time the scientists call "revolution," when the water freezes at the poles and great glaciers form, making the earth cold over a large portion.

"Normal" times are times of low relief. Mountains appear in the periods of "revolution." Mountains always connect with cold. They are one of the causes of cold weather. Mountains gradually wear away, the earth becomes more level and warm, uniform weather prevails. That is the story of the ages. It would take actually millions of years for this to happen naturally; prophecy indicates that it is to be done suddenly. The earth is to be redeemed, not by some slow, natural process, but by sudden, drastic acts of God.

What nature would do in the course of time, God will do at once. There is a very definite time limit placed upon the process of restoration. It is to be all done in one generation. The geologists have discovered from the rocks, lake beds, trees, coal beds, etc., what the normal earth is like that God originally made. Revelation and the prophets tell what is to be. They correspond.

A warm climate over all the earth, a water canopy far above the earth, and absence of high mountains are the main physical features, both of the scientists and of the Bible. The prophets tell how this is to be accomplished. The ice will melt, the oceans will rise, the terrific heat will evaporate the extra water reforming the canopy of Genesis. In the original form, water stood above the firmament (sky) and below the firmament.

Then, the final feature of normal times: the mountains will be scattered, the perpetual hills will bow.

Revelation 16
20 And every island fled away, and the mountains were not found.

Ezekiel 38
19 Surely in that day there shall be a great shaking in the land of Israel;
20 So that the fishes of the sea, and the fowls of the heaven, and the beasts of the field, and all creeping things that creep upon the earth, and all the men that are upon the face of the earth, shall shake at my presence, and the mountains shall be thrown down, and the steep places shall fall, and every wall shall fall to the ground.

The Tribulation

Habakkuk 3
7 I saw the tents of Cushan in affliction: and the curtains of the land of Midian did tremble.

This is the poetic way of indicating what is commonly called the tribulation. Cushan is Cush, or Ethiopia; the "an" is added to make it correspond with Midian, for poetic effect. This is what Daniel called the time of trouble such as never was since there was a nation (Dan. 12:1), and what Jesus referred to as "the beginning of sorrows" (Matt. 24:8).

Habakkuk immediately goes on to explain his meaning.

Habakkuk 3
8 Was the Lord displeased against the rivers? was thine anger against the rivers? was thy wrath against the sea, that thou didst ride upon thine horses and thy chariots of salvation?

Notice the four elements in the tribulation: three

of wrath and one of grace. This is an expansion of the petition in the beginning of the prayer: "O Lord, revive thy work in the midst of the years, in the midst of the years make known: in wrath remember mercy."

It is at this point that Habakkuk begins to associate wrath and mercy. There are three elements of wrath and one of mercy. As the word is used in Revelation, "tribulation" does not apply to the entire time between the resurrection and the return of Christ with His saints, but only the first part. During the first part of this time wrath is poured out from heaven, but it is mixed with grace and a great number of people (sometimes called "Tribulation Saints") are saved, a multitude which no man could number of all nations, and kindreds, and people, and tongues, together with a hundred and forty-four thousand of Israel.

This is the work of the four horsemen (Rev. 6). This is when God in the midst of wrath remembers mercy. Again, we have the number four. Three of them have to do with wrath, and one with grace. The second, third and fourth horsemen are involved in war, famine, and pestilence; the first horseman is in charge of the preaching of the gospel, but all four may be said to ride upon horses and chariots of salvation, because they are all employed in the same program of redemption.

The function of the four horsemen is to produce the great number of saved that come out of this time of tribulation. Jesus gave us the same summary of that time of tribulation. He said, "All these are the beginning of sorrows" (Matt. 24).

The things He mentioned are identical with the operation of the four horsemen.

"For nation shall rise against nation, and kingdom against kingdom." The second horseman takes peace from the earth.

"There shall be famines." The third horseman is a food adminstrator whose work is to keep people from starving when peace is taken from the earth.

"And pestilences." The fourth horseman kills with the beasts and animals of the earth.

"And earthquakes, in divers places." ("In divers places" modifies all the foregoing judgments.) These earthquakes are recorded in the last part of the sixth chapter of Revelation, when the sixth seal is opened.

Then the Lord mentions the tribulation saints: "Then shall they deliver you up to be afflicted, and shall kill you: and ye shall be hated of all nations for my name's sake." These saints are the result of the work of the first horseman: "And this gospel of the kingdom shall be preached in all the world for a witness unto all nations; and then shall the end of the dispensation come."

These four horsemen operate as a group. They have one purpose—to cause the conversion of that great number from every nation. The sixth chapter of Revelation pictures this work as it is seen from heaven. The four horsemen are sent out from heaven by one of the four living ones, following the opening of the seals, by Christ himself. This is a heavenly administration which directly connects with the earth, for this is the day when heaven is dealing with the earth in a very definite and commanding way.

How will all this appear to the people on the earth? They, of course, would not see the seals being opened; they would not hear the command of the living ones to the horsemen; they would not see the four horsemen in the same way they would be seen in heaven because spiritual things cannot be seen with mortal eyes except by special arrangement.

However, they will be seen from the earth—and heard. This story is told in the 14th chapter of Revelation. To understand it you have only to know the meaning of "angel" in the Bible. The word means messenger. It is often used of angelic beings who were always heavenly beings. But it is also used of people, and sometimes of Christ, when they assume the part of messengers of God.

The messengers, or ministers, of the seven churches are called angels: "Unto the angel of the church of Ephesus write," etc. The angels that have the seven last plagues, the trumpets and vials, twice say that they are of the saints. This can be seen by comparing:

Revelation 17

1 And there came one of the seven angels which had the seven vials, and talked with me, saying unto me, Come hither; I will shew unto thee the judgment of the great whore that sitteth upon many waters:

with the following verses:

Revelation 19

9 And he saith unto me, Write, Blessed are they which are called unto the marriage supper of the Lamb. And he saith unto me, These are the true sayings of God.

10 And I fell at his feet to worship him. And he said unto me, See thou do it not: I am thy fellowservant, and of thy brethren that have the testimony of Jesus: worship God: for the testimony of Jesus is the spirit of prophecy.

Revelation 22

8 And I John saw these things, and heard them. And when I had heard and seen, I fell down to worship before the feet of the angel which shewed me these things.

9 Then saith he unto me, See thou do it not: for I am thy fellowservant, and of thy brethren the prophets, and of them which keep the sayings of this book: worship God.

So we read in

Revelation 14

6 And I saw another angel [messenger] fly in the midst of heaven, having the everlasting gospel to preach unto them that dwell on the earth, and to every nation, and kindred, and tongue, and people.

This gospel is the same gospel that we preach except that it is suited to the times. It is the gospel of faith in Christ.

Revelation 14

12 Here is the patience [steadfastness] of the saints: here are they that keep the commandments of God, and the faith of Jesus.

This gospel is preached during the tribulation period when Antichrist is persecuting the saints. Jesus put it in the same time. "Then shall they deliver you up to be afflicted . . . and because iniquity shall abound, the love of many shall wax cold." It is during this time that the gospel is preached to every kindred, tongue, people and nation, according to Revelation; and it is at this time that "this gospel of the kingdom shall be preached in all the world," according to Jesus (Matt. 24:14).

The tribulation gospel is suited to the tribulation. It deals with the conditions that face the people, especially the believers.

Revelation 14

7 Saying with a loud voice, Fear God, and give glory to him; for the hour of his judgment is come: and worship him that made heaven, and earth, and the sea, and the fountains of waters.

Other messengers follow; one of them warns against receiving the mark of the beast.

Revelation 14

9 And the third angel [messenger] followed them,

saying with a loud voice, If any man worship the beast and his image, and receive his mark in his forehead, or in his hand,

10 The same shall drink of the wine of the wrath of God, which is poured out without mixture into the cup of his indignation; and he shall be tormented with fire and brimstone in the presence of the holy angels, and in the presence of the Lamb.

These messengers must be saints because the saints are the only ones commissioned to preach the gospel. This is a part of the work of the saints after the resurrection. It is the work of the four horsemen who are sent forth from heaven when Christ breaks the seals. The result of this work is told in the 7th chapter— a great multitude saved from every nation, people and tongue. That is the extent of the preaching of the messengers from heaven—to every kindred, tongue, people, and nation.

This will not be done twice, so we know it all refers to the same process. Jesus said it will not be done twice. He said, "Then shall the end come." The reason we do not read of Antichrist in the 6th and 7th chapters of Revelation is that the action is in heaven and the result is on the earth. Antichrist is not the result of heavenly administration. He is not sent out with a commission from heaven. He is not the result of the breaking of a seal.

Chapters 12 to 16 tell the same story, but from the standpoint of the earth. There you do not read of the seals or the horsemen, but you do see what the people on the earth see: Antichrist, the image, the mark, and the angels preaching the gospel through the heavens. What are horsemen in heaven appear as angels to the earth. The people on the earth see heavenly beings only as they are revealed to them and in the way they are revealed to them. This has always been so.

During Antichrist's savage campaign against the saints, it will be impossible to preach the gospel on the earth, or to hold any services whatsoever. The gospel will be preached, but it will be preached from heaven by those who are caught up at the resurrection. This is how God in wrath remembers mercy.

Habakkuk 3
9 Thy bow was made quite naked, according to the oaths of the tribes, even thy word.

The original text, here, has not been perfectly preserved. An exact translation is almost impossible. A bow is made to represent the Word of God, the gospel, in accordance with God's promises to the tribes of Israel. The gospel has its roots in the Old Testament. It is a carrying out of the promises God made to Israel. This preaching mentioned here by Habakkuk and by the Olivet Discourse and Revelation is also the beginning of the conversion of Israel, for it is then that the hundred and forty-four thousand Israelites are saved and sealed. They are the firstfruits of the new kingdom, which will be established when Christ comes and all Israel is saved.

This bow is also mentioned in Revelation. The first horseman, who rides a white horse, carries a bow. Habakkuk 3, which runs parallel to Revelation 6 all the way through, also mentions the bow and says it is the Word.

(I am well aware of the common interpretation of this verse, Rev. 6:2, which says this first horseman is a counterfeit; and the white, the bow, the crown, and the final victory should all be read in reverse, as though they mean the opposite of what they usually mean in Scripture. There is nothing in the context to suggest that. He is sent forth by one of the four living ones. Are the living ones also counterfeit?)

Revelation 5

14 And the four beasts [living ones] said, Amen. And the four and twenty elders fell down and worshipped him that liveth for ever and ever.

Should this verse also be taken in reverse? Are the elders to represent false worshippers? Is all of Revelation to be read in reverse? What kind of interpretation are we being subjected to? Nobody would see Antichrist coming out of heaven, commissioned by Christ, riding a white horse, carrying the Word, wearing a crown and going forth to conquer unless he had Antichrist in mind and were trying to find a place to fit him in. A straightforward interpretation, without some preconceived notion, would never find Antichrist in that verse. The inconsistency of such an interpretation is immediately apparent when you consider that there are four horsemen and only one Antichrist. To make the first horseman a man and the others such impersonal things as war, famine and death is so inconsistent that it is not worthy of our consideration. If the first one is a wicked man, then the others are men, even more wicked. When you read the 6th chapter of Revelation, begin with the last verse of the 5th chapter and put the scene where it belongs—in heaven.

Now we come to a detail that is not specifically mentioned in Revelation, but without Revelation we would not be able to construct the whole story. Revelation deals with the future of the saints. Their work in heaven has a direct result on the earth, and those details are given us in Revelation. Now we come to an event that has a natural cause on this earth and is not directly the result of any heavenly administration. It is therefore not noted in Revelation. Many of the prophets saw the flood mentioned here by Habakkuk. It is not unusual for Revelation to omit details not directly connected with the saints: for instance, the Davidic Kingdom, the part of the Jews in the Battle of Armageddon, the return of the Jews, etc. Even Antichrist is mentioned only in his relationship to the saints. For all other details, which are many, you have to go to the Old Testament prophets.

Habakkuk 3
9 Thou didst cleave the earth with rivers.

The Pulpit Commentary says: "This refers to some catastrophe like that which happened at the flood, when the foundations of the great deep were broken up." This is the same flood mentioned by the other prophets, and, according to Jeremiah will come out of the north.

Jeremiah 47
2 Thus saith the Lord; Behold, waters rise up out of the north, and shall be an overflowing flood, and shall overflow the land, and all that is therein; the city, and them that dwell therein: then the men shall cry, and all the inhabitants of the land shall howl.

It will be, according to Amos, not a flood caused by rain, but a flood caused by a rising of the sea.

Amos 9
6 It is he that buildeth his stories in the heaven, and hath founded his troop in the earth; he that calleth for the waters of the sea, and poureth them out upon the face of the earth: The Lord is his name.

Noah's flood was caused partly by water coming out of the sky. That water has been stored up at the poles. It will leave the poles, come back over the earth, and then be returned to the sky by the great heat of the seven last plagues.

Not all of the water of Noah's flood came from the sky. Some came out of the earth. That water probably went back to the earth or stayed in the oceans, making them much larger than the original seas. The present amount of surplus water is not nearly enough to cause another universal flood. Only the seacoast and low countries would be flooded. It will not cover the earth as did the deluge. The rainbow is the seal of God's promise never again to destroy all mankind off the face of the earth.

The melting of the ice at the poles, especially the North Pole, would do some strange things. One of those things would be the rising of the crust of the earth when the weight of the ice is removed. This would cause rivers to flow in opposite directions and bring a flood of waters from the north [in the Northern Hemisphere].

Habakkuk 3
10 The moutains saw thee, and they trembled: the overflowing of the water passed by: the deep uttered his voice, and lifted up his hands on high.

Literally, the mountains were in pain. To this we should add:

Revelation 6
12 And I beheld when he had opened the sixth seal, and, lo, there was a great earthquake; and the sun became black as sackcloth of hair, and the moon became as blood;

13 And the stars of heaven fell unto the earth, even as a fig tree casteth her untimely figs, when she is shaken of a mighty wind.

14 And the heaven departed as a scroll when it is rolled together; and every mountain and island were moved out of their places.

If the earth should get warm gradually and the ice should melt slowly, it would take a long time, possibly thousands of years, to melt all the ice. As the water rose, generation after generation, the people would gradually move back, or build dikes. It would not cause any sudden disaster. However, the fact is, man is learning how to control climate; and what might take even millions of years of natural change could now be done almost overnight.

Man, by himself, will possibly not get that opportunity, because God has some plans of His own. It has been noted in the science sections of news magazines that a few well-placed bombs on Greenland would break up that ice pack with the result that the ocean would rise twelve feet. Greenland has 700,000 square miles of ice reaching up to a mile and a half high. This, if melted, would put New York, Philadelphia, and Washington under water. It could be done now with atom bombs. Of course, we have no intention of bombing Greenland, but this shows what would happen if the falling stars mentioned in Revelation should strike Greenland, breaking up the ice faster than atom bombs could ever do. When God begins to shake the earth so that islands and mountains are moved out of their places, the ice could break up so fast that the flood mentioned by the prophets would sweep down across the earth.

Habakkuk associates earthquakes with the coming flood and poetically speaks of the deep uttering his voice and lifting up his hands on high.

Habakkuk 3

11 The sun and moon stood still in their habitation: at the light of thine arrows they went, and at the shining of thy glittering spear.

As we have noted before, the poles turned cold suddenly. The reason the North Pole is cold is that the earth is tipped on its axis some 23 degrees, which brings darkness in the north for six months of the year. If the ice suddenly froze, then the earth must have suddenly tipped. (That the ice suddenly froze is proved by the well-preserved flesh of animals found in it when it melts.)

There is too much water on the earth. This extra water has been here since the Flood. It was then that the windows of heaven were opened and the water came down. Prior to that time there was a great canopy of water around the earth at a great height. In order to restore a perfect heaven and a perfect earth, this canopy of water must be restored. It has been preserved as ice during these many years.

Not all the ice would melt at once. The flood will be under control. God will have a way of taking care of the surplus water. Revelation tells that story.

If the earth should suddenly begin to right itself when the weight is shifted because of the melting ice, it would, in the words of Isaiah, "reel like a drunkard."

Isaiah 24

18 And it shall come to pass, that he who fleeth from the noise of the fear shall fall into the pit; and he that cometh up out of the midst of the pit shall be taken in the snare: for the windows from on high are open, and the foundations of the earth do shake.

19 The earth is utterly broken down, the earth is clean dissolved, the earth is moved exceedingly.

20 The earth shall reel to and fro like a drunkard.

23 Then the moon shall be confounded, and the sun ashamed, when the Lord of hosts shall reign in mount Zion, and in Jerusalem, and before his ancients gloriously.

About seven years seem to be covered by these events. Great earthquakes are noted also at the time of the return of Christ. It will require all of the seven last plagues to bring the water under control and restore it to its original place. Great convulsions are noted at the beginning and at the end of this series of earth-shaking events. It is no wonder Jesus said that except these days should be shortened, no flesh would be saved.

Such a movement of the earth would cause some

strange sights in the sky. In some places the sun would rise when it should set; in some places the sun would seem to stand still; and in some places the sun would suddenly set. Can we find all three phenomena in prophecy?

Zechariah speaks of it being daylight when it should be dark.

Zechariah 14

7 But it shall come to pass, that at evening time it shall be light.

Habakkuk mentions the sun and moon standing still.

Habakkuk 3

11 The sun and moon stood still in their habitation.

This does not refer to Joshua's day. The other things mentioned did not happen then. This is prophecy.

The third is found in Amos.

Amos 8

9 And it shall come to pass in that day, saith the Lord God, that I will cause the sun to go down at noon, and I will darken the earth in the clear day.

Habakkuk 3

12 Thou didst march through the land in indignation, thou didst thresh the heathen (nations) in anger.

13 Thou wentest forth for the salvation of thy people, even for salvation with thine anointed.

Here again we have the two elements of wrath and salvation going hand in hand. God's wrath will be very much in evidence. When the four horsemen are sent forth to do their work in the world, and when the stars fall and the heavens and the earth shake, the people on the earth will know about God sitting on His judgment throne and the Lamb breaking the seals and sending these things upon the earth, for they will say to the mountains and rocks:

Revelation 6

16 Fall on us, and hide us from the face of him that sitteth on the throne, and from the wrath of the Lamb:

17 For the great day of his wrath is come; and who shall be able to stand?

How do they know this? The answer is at hand. The work of the first horseman is to proclaim the Word:

Revelation 14

7 Saying with a loud voice, Fear God, and give glory to him; for the hour of his judgment is come: and worship him that made heaven, and earth, and the sea, and the fountains of waters.

This is the day when God's wrath is in the world, but it is (at first) mixed with grace so that the main purpose of the wrath is the salvation of people. This is the great feature of the tribulation period (but not necessarily of the seven last plagues which follow).

Habakkuk 3

13 Thou woundedst the head out of the house of the wicked, by discovering the foundation unto the neck.

Here Habakkuk poetically pays his respects to Antichrist. The house of the wicked is the kingdom of the beast. The head of the house will be wounded, even destroyed. The rest of the kingdom, from the neck down, will also be destroyed. First the head is wounded, then the rest of the body is destroyed.

First, Antichrist and the false prophet will be taken, then their kingdom will be taken over by the destruction of their armies.

Revelation 19

19 And I saw the beast, and the kings of the earth, and their armies, gathered together to make war against him that sat on the horse, and against his army.

20 And the beast was taken, and with him the false prophet that wrought miracles before him, with which

he deceived them that had received the mark of the beast, and them that worshipped his image. These both were cast alive into a lake of fire burning with brimstone.

21 And the remnant were slain with the sword of him that sat upon the horse, which sword proceeded out of his mouth: and all the fowls were filled with their flesh.

Habakkuk 3

14 Thou didst strike through with his staves the head of his villages: they came out as a whirlwind to scatter me: their rejoicing was as to devour the poor secretly.

There is difficulty in arriving at the meaning of "villages." The Septuagint renders it "mighty men." Others translate it "army," "warriors," "hordes," "rulers," "judges."

Habakkuk means that the armies of Antichrist will destroy themselves. "Thou didst strike through with *his* staves the head of *his* warriors." They will strike their own men with their own weapons.

This is in harmony with the other prophecies concerning the battle of Armageddon. For instance:

Zechariah 14

13 And it shall come to pass in that day, that a great tumult from the Lord shall be among them; and they shall lay hold every one on the hand of his neighbour, and his hand shall rise up against the hand of his neighbour.

Ezekiel 38

21 And I will call for a sword against him throughout all my mountains, saith the Lord God: every man's sword shall be against his brother.

Haggai 2

22 And I will overthrow the throne of kingdoms, and I will destroy the strength of the kingdoms of the

heathen [nations]; and I will overthrow the chariots, and those that ride in them; and the horses and their riders shall come down, every one by the sword of his brother.

Habakkuk 3

14 They came out as a whirlwind to scatter me: their rejoicing was as to devour the poor secretly.

15 Thou didst walk through the sea with thine horses, through the heap of great waters.

God speaks through the prophet: "They came out as a whirlwind to scatter me." The nations will gather with great speed to try to prevent the reign of Christ. "And I saw the beast, and the kings of the earth, and their armies, gathered together to make war against him that sat on the horse, and against his army" (Rev. 19:19).

Ezekiel 38

9 Thou shalt ascend and come like a storm, thou shalt be like a cloud to cover the land, thou, and all thy bands, and many people with thee.

10 Thus saith the Lord God; It shall also come to pass, that at the same time shall things come into thy mind, and thou shalt think an evil thought:

11 And thou shalt say, I will go up to the land of unwalled villages; I will go to them that are at rest, that dwell safely, all of them dwelling without walls, and having neither bars nor gates,

12 To take a spoil, and to take a prey.

That is when Christ appears on a white horse.

Revelation 19

11 And I saw heaven opened, and behold a white horse; and he that sat upon him was called Faithful and True, and in righteousness he doth judge and make war.

14 And the armies which were in heaven followed him upon white horses.

Habakkuk 3

16 When I heard, my belly trembled; my lips quivered at the voice: rottenness entered into my bones, and I trembled in myself, that I might rest in the day of trouble: when he cometh up unto the people, he will invade them with his troops.

Habakkuk, in conclusion, expresses his feelings when he contemplates the vision: "My innermost part, my inward self, trembled with fear. My lips quivered with fear at the voice of God that sounded in me, proclaiming these awful judgments."

"That I might rest in the day of trouble," the *Pulpit Commentary* translates: "I who shall rest in the day of tribulation," and comments: "The prophet suddenly expresses his confidence that he shall have rest in this affliction; amid this terror and awe he is sure that there remaineth a rest for the people of God."

It is not clear whether the invasion mentioned here is that of Christ and the saints, about which the prophet has been talking, or whether he means the invasion of Antichrist at the battle of Armageddon. Both are in view. The next verse would seem to indicate that the invasion of Antichrist is referred to, because of the accompanying circumstances.

Habakkuk 3

17 Although the fig tree shall not blossom, neither shall fruit be in the vines; the labour of the olive shall fail, and the fields shall yield no meat; the flock shall be cut off from the fold, and there shall be no herd in the stalls:

This situation always follows in the wake of an invasion. It will be even more extreme in this case because the announced purpose of the invasion is to take a prey and a spoil. The land will be stripped bare by the invaders.

Habakkuk 3

18 Yet I will rejoice in the Lord, I will joy in the God of my salvation.

19 The Lord God is my strength, and he will make my feet like hinds' feet, and he will make me to walk upon mine high places.

The emphasis is on the word "I." Others will go through the tribulation, I will be caught up to my high place. Thus Habakkuk puts himself in the place of the saints who have the "blessed hope."

4

The New Heavens and the New Earth

The Time Is Short

In the closing pages of the 1954 report of the *National Science Foundation* is this startling statement:

> Glacier studies have given clear indications that we are now in a cycle of warming which began about 1900. It is estimated that if the indicated warming continues for another twenty-five to fifty years, the ice will melt out of the Arctic Ocean in the summer, making it navigable.
>
> In addition, the warming cycle, if continued, may melt enough ice now tied up in glaciers to add to the sea level sufficiently to affect the lives of millions of people living along low coastal lands.

A large amount of work has been done in the fields of climatology and meteorology. Volumes have been written. Some experts have warned us far in advance what a slight change in an average temperature would mean to the world.

A scientific book, *Climate Through the Ages* by C.E.P. Brooks was reviewed by Richard J. Russell, professor of Physical Geography, Louisiana State University, in a book called *Climate and Man* which is a Yearbook of the Department of Agriculture (1941). Professor Russell says:

Geologic Climates

There are two broad types of climatic patterns indicated by the geologic record, the normal and the glacial.

The characteristic of glacial climates is the existence of frozen seas during the summer in polar regions. Such is the case today. The absence of polar ice is the characteristic of normal times from the geological standpoint. The difference between glacial and normal climates is sharply defined, and transitions from one to the other occupied inconsequential intervals of time. It is probable that less than one percent of geologic time has experienced glacial climatic patterns.

Normal geologic periods were times of quiet between revolutions during which normal climates prevailed. Rocks deposited at such times indicate a minimum of relief—unevenness in height—and few signs of crustal unrest. The paleontologic record is one of widespread ranges in both plant and animal distribution. The early Cenozoic was such a time. Plants closely allied to some of our warm-climate types were flourishing in places such as Greenland, Spitzbergen, and other lands in high latitudes where their growth is impossible today. Even more strikingly uniform were the temperatures in all latitudes during most of the Paleozoic and Mesozoic eras.

For a planet to have an experience characterized by alternations between normal and glacial climatic patterns, its surface must be covered by extensive oceans, and the temperature of its polar regions must remain not far from the freezing temperature of water. Only the earth among the planets falls within the slight range in these essential requirements. The sharp contrast between glacial and normal climates is a reflection of the sharp discontinuity between liquid water and solid ice. Water is penetrated for a considerable distance by solar radiation and thus slowly becomes warmer. Ocean currents and convection spread temperature effects widely. The marine influences in climate are well known, the most significant effect being the tendency toward uniformity of temperature. Ice is fixed in position and in many ways resembles land surface from the climatic standpoint. The effect of an open arctic ocean is that of adding area to marine climatic influences, but a polar icecap has a different climatic effect similar to an addition of continental area, which makes for comparatively rapid and violent changes in temperature. The balance is so delicate in terrestrial climatic patterns that a swing from one condition to the other—a polar icecap or no polar icecap—means the change from normal to glacial climates for the whole of the earth's surface.

Brooks has shown that a surprisingly small variation in temperature causes a change from open to ice-capped polar seas. As long as winter temperatures remain above 28 degrees F., the approximate freezing point of ocean water, the polar seas remain open. At slightly lower temperatures, the ice frozen during the winter melts again in the following summer, and the seas remain effectively open. But if the winter temperature falls about 5 degrees F. lower than the freezing point of ocean water, an icecap will form. Its growth will be slow at first, but summer melting will not quite offset the effect of winter freezing. After its radius has reached about 600 miles, the growth of the icecap becomes rapid because the ice itself has a cooling effect on surrounding areas, and the rate of summer melting is thus reduced. Growth continues until the ice extends so far from the polar areas that its margins encounter temperatures sufficiently high to stop further extension. Glacial climates have their optimum development at such times. Rising temperatures cause retreat of the ice and the modification of climatic patterns. The cooling effect of the icecap is so great that retreat is slow until the ice has diminished in area to its critical point —a radius of about 600 miles—after which the ice disappears very rapidly.

Two Degrees

Polar ice now lowers the temperatures in Canada and the United States many degrees. It profoundly affects ocean temperatures, especially at great depths. There is a sort of vicious circle in icecap and temperature relationships. Brooks calculates that lowering of polar temperatures 5 degrees F. under the freezing points ultimately results in a drop of 50 degrees F. in polar winter temperatures. The initial drop causes the growth of the polar icecap; the cooling effect of the ice itself is responsible for the remainder of the drop. A rise of 2 degrees F. in the temperature of the earth now would be sufficient to clear polar seas of all ice. We are thus in a world where the balance is extremely delicate between normal and glacial climates.

During most of geologic time mountains were low, seas widespread, and normal climates prevalent. Extremely low winter temperatures were unknown, even in the central parts of continents in high latitudes. Distinctions between tropical and polar regions were less evident than at present, the cooling toward higher latitudes being gradual over both oceans and continents. Climatic zones of animal and plant life existed, but the contrasts between zones were not great. Polar air covered the highest latitudes, but its outrushes toward the equator were less sharp than those today, and the temperatures carried by its winds were by no means so low because the polar air mass was much more restricted in extent and developed over regions neither ice-covered nor near any polar icecap. All temperature boundaries were shifted poleward, so that subpolar lands experienced conditions about like those of today's temperate zones, and middle latitudes were subtropical. At the same time, the tropics themselves were probably only slightly warmer than at present.

A rise of two degrees in the world's overall climate

would not be noticed at the start. It would take a number of years before any difference would be felt.

The following is from the *Chicago Daily News:*

> The climate, which is the cumulative record of the weather over a period of years, decades and centuries, seems to be changing. As climate changes go, it is happening at a rapid rate.
>
> Fifty years from now, winters in most parts of the United States and even some of Canada may be marked by only occasional short freezes. These are estimates made on the basis of the work of some of the best scientific minds in America.
>
> Since the U.S. Weather Bureau began collecting reliable figures from all over the country, about 60 years ago, the normal mean temperature has climbed by about two degrees.
>
> Two degrees may not sound like much. But scientists believe that an increase only that great all over the world would be enough to melt every scrap of ice at both the North and South Poles.
>
> That much melted ice would raise the levels of the oceans of the world by 180 feet.
>
> Here are some of the important developments that scientists note with the trend toward warmer weather: In Greenland the ice has retreated beyond limits it is known to have occupied for 500 years. In the Southwest continued water shortage is partly due to man's own impact on the land. But climatologists believe the extended nature of the drought has a direct tie with the melting of the Arctic ice pack 3,000 miles to the north.
>
> In Canada almost every year farmers push the boundary of wheat culture northward. A longer growing season, milder winters, and hardier plants combine to supply the reasons. There is little danger, however, that Americans will have to abandon any region merely because it gets too hot.
>
> But there is one real danger to industry and to agriculture—drought. Most of the scientists who are

predicting warmer weather believe that the water shortages in the Southwest will spread farther and farther north and east. If the water table falls still further below the surface, and the streams continue to dry up in the summer, the industrial boom that has hit the Southwest since World War II may slacken. Only one area in the country has an assured permanent supply of fresh water for unlimited use. That is the Great Lakes basin, located around the largest reservoir in the world.

Cleveland, Ohio, now has an average winter temperature that used to be typical of Cincinnati. Cincinnati has climbed to the old Washington level of 35.5 degrees, and the Washington January average has risen to 39 degrees.

In the North Sea the temperature is up four degrees and is changing the types of marine vegetation.

The farther north you go the greater is the rate of change. In some parts of the Arctic the temperature has risen as much as 20 degrees.

The Ocean Is Beginning to Rise

According to a report of the U.S. Coast and Geodetic Survey, the ocean along the Atlantic coast has risen about half a foot in the past 50 years, but the greater part of that rise has come in the last 15 years. The rate of rise is increasing. (New York at the Battery is only four feet above sea level at high tide.)

Countries like Norway, which were almost paralyzed by a sudden lack of fish because the fish had moved north, are now enjoying a boom. Fish from the south have moved in and the fishermen have built bigger boats to go farther north. They gain both ways.

William J. Baxter in *Warmer Weather—Boom in North* (International Economic Research Bureau, New York, N.Y.) under a paragraph heading, "It's Later

Than We Think," says: "Our studies indicate that the movement of the heat zone northward is far more rapid than generally understood."

Isaiah Saw It Coming

Now it is beginning to appear in print—the thing I have been looking for. Mr. Baxter says it in his report: "The rapid melting of the century-old ice is not only creating a mounting sea level all over the world, but even more important, I am convinced (like two scientists from the Scripps Institute) that it is affecting the rotation of the earth."

This could be the cause of both earthquakes and signs in the heavens, so prominent in prophecy.

Isaiah 24
18 The foundations of the earth do shake.
19 The earth is utterly broken down, the earth is clean dissolved, the earth is moved exceedingly.
20 The earth shall reel to and fro like a drunkard.

The New Heaven and the New Earth

In order that we may get the subject clearly before us, let us bring together the main features as they have been presented so far.

The original heaven and earth as they appear in the book of Genesis were composed of water in the sky above the earth, air between the water and the earth, and, on the earth, seas, but no great oceans. There was more land and less water than we have now.

At the time of the Flood, additional water came to the earth. Normally the water system of the earth operates in a closed circuit. No water comes down that has not first gone up. The same amount that goes up, comes down, so that the amount of water remains the same. So, in order to cover the entire earth with water as in the Flood, additional water would have to be provided. This additional water came from that great canopy of water that Genesis says was above the firmament.

There is now too much water on the earth. A portion of the surplus water was suddenly frozen at the poles so that it could not return and flood the earth. God has reserved this surplus water (as He told Job) for His own use in His own time.

That time is the end of this age, and there are many indications that the day is approaching. The balance between water and ice is so close that a change of only two or three degrees in the temperature of the world would be sufficient to start a melting of the ice which represents the surplus water that came down at the Flood.

The climate of the earth is now changing to such an extent that the situation becomes alarming. Civilization could hardly survive a two-degree rise in the world's temperature.

On the other hand, we have Bible prophecy. There is nothing in the Bible to indicate that civilization is going to face any such crisis.

In a very peculiar sense this surplus water belongs to God. He put it in the heavens. He opened the windows of heaven and sent the water down to the earth; then He stored this extra water at the poles and set bars and gates and said, "Hitherto shalt thou come, but no further" (Job 38:11).

This water will be used to produce a sudden flood upon certain places, at a certain time; but it will not remain permanently upon the earth; for, in the new heavens and the new earth, John said: "And there was no more sea" (Rev. 21:1).

1

The earth of Genesis. Firmament separating the waters from the waters.

2

The Flood. Water above the firmament coming down.

3

Water rushing to the poles to be held there by freezing.

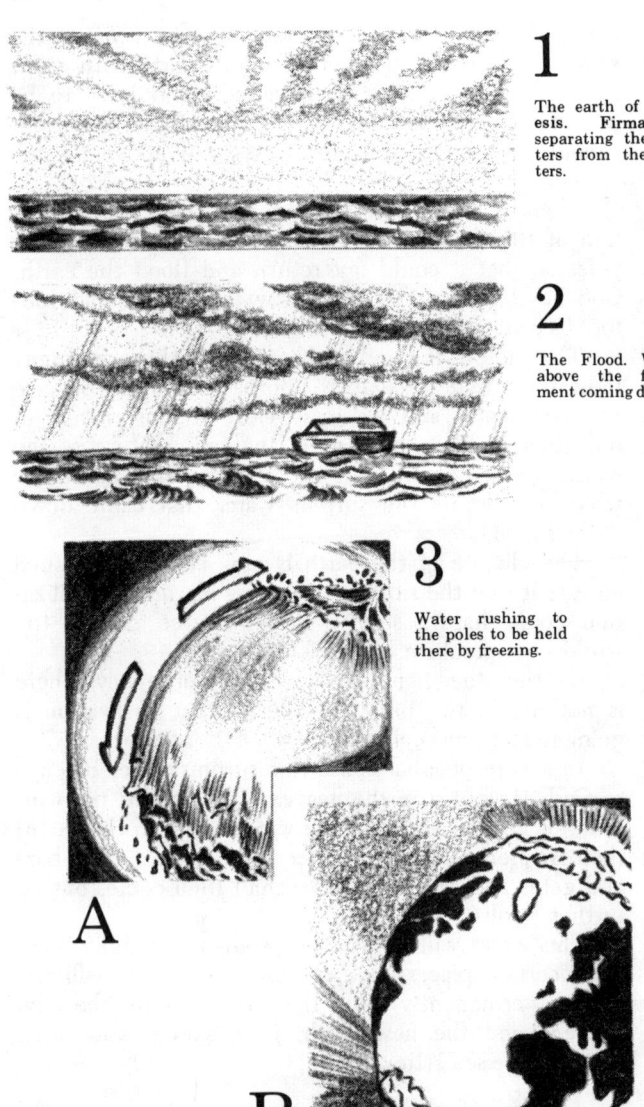

A

B

4

Ice melting causing another flood along coastal lands.

5

Fire and heat evaporate the water restoring the canopy of Genesis.

The changing climate does not mean that the ice will melt slowly, year after year, until the ocean rises and covers a large portion of the civilized world, as the scientists say it will. It means only that we are approaching the end of the age—the Day of the Lord—when God will take over the disposition of the surplus water.

This will be done according to prophecy. We have the prophecies. They all point to the same time when God will hasten the melting of the ice, bombarding it with falling stars and breaking it up with earthquakes.

This will cause a sudden flood. This flood is mentioned in some of the prophecies concerning the coastal lands.

It will then be necessary to force all this surplus water back into the sky. This could be done only by heat—great heat.

This brings us to the final stage of the process, which is reported in Revelation.

The Restoration of the Earth

Making the new heaven and the new earth is a somewhat different process from that which is recorded in Genesis. In the former instance God merely destroyed and made new; now we are in a process of redemption. There is a vast difference. This time the earth is not to be completely destroyed and made over again, but is to be redeemed. Redemption will take more time, but it will be worth it, because the result will be an everlasting kingdom, "world without end" (Isa. 45:17).

Perfection must be established, but it must be established without destroying anything that can be redeemed. God could destroy the heavens and the earth and make new ones, but that would not be redemption. That is what happened before.

If God is to redeem the earth, He must restore to its original perfection everything that is good, and destroy only that which cannot be redeemed.

The book of Revelation is the book of redemption, not the destruction of the earth. At this writing we are concerned only with that part of redemption which refers to water.

Now we are faced with two facts, one present and one future. We know that there is enough water on the earth to raise the oceans enough to cover a large portion of the best land to an extent that would threaten civilization itself. We know also that in the end there will be no more sea; that the ocean will be dried up to the extent that much more land will appear. What will happen between these two conditions? What will dispose of the water?

First the ice will have to be melted. The fact that that is happening now is the most sensational thing that has happened to date toward the fulfillment of prophecy. It indicates that a process has started that cannot continue beyond certain limits before God takes over.

Next the water will have to be disposed of. Heat will evaporate water and pull it into the sky. To break up the ice quickly, we require earthquakes and falling stars. The prophecies of these are found in the sixth chapter of Revelation (quoted previously).

To evaporate the water we require heat. This is found in the eighth chapter of Revelation, which we will examine now.

Heat and Still More Heat

Revelation 8

7 The first angel sounded, and there followed hail and fire mingled with blood, and they were cast

upon the earth: and the third part of trees was burnt up, and all green grass was burnt up.

How much heat is required to burn green grass? Any brush fire would be stopped by a field of green grass. This fire is general over at least one-third of the earth. Hail and fire are a strange combination (unless the hail is composed of white hot stones). If all the green grass is burnt up, the earth would seem to be on fire. The heat will be tremendous.

Revelation 8

8 And the second angel sounded, and as it were a great mountain burning with fire was cast into the sea: and the third part of the sea became blood;

9 And the third part of the creatures which were in the sea, and had life, died; and the third part of the ships were destroyed.

John saw a mountain burning with fire. That is difficult to conceive but the meaning is clear. Something big comes down out of the sky into the ocean which causes it to become hot, so hot that one-third of the creatures in the sea die, probably those which are not able to go deep enough to find cool water.

The water will be so hot that it will destroy one-third of the ships that are in the sea. In no case is the fire universal; only one-third of the earth and one-third of the sea are directly affected at one time. The reason for this is at once apparent. This is redemption, not total destruction, and therefore it must be carried on in a way that will not completely destroy all life upon the earth. In time, the entire earth must be purged.

This fire may have more than one purpose. We are concerned now only with one feature, the disposition of the surplus water. It might also be noted that during this time, no wind will blow.

Revelation 7
1 And after these things I saw four angels standing on the four corners of the earth, holding the four winds of the earth, that the wind should not blow on the earth, nor on the sea, nor on any tree.

The water that is evaporated will go straight up and stay there. This is a remarkable feature. We know now—but John could not have known it—that prolonged hot spells generate cyclones which draw up large amounts of water. This water is sometimes carried over land along the coast and then is suddenly deposited, causing disastrous floods. In this case the forces of nature are restrained, miraculously. The cyclones are prevented from forming; the moisture is not allowed to return to the earth.

Revelation 8
10 And the third angel sounded, and there fell a great star from heaven, burning as it were a lamp, and it fell upon the third part of the rivers, and upon the fountains of waters.

The primary purpose of this judgment is to punish those who have persecuted the saints.

Revelation 16
4 And the third angel poured out his vial upon the rivers and fountains of waters; and they became blood.

5 And I heard the angel of the waters say, Thou art righteous, O Lord, which art, and wast, and shalt be, because thou hast judged thus.

6 For they have shed the blood of saints and prophets, and thou hast given them blood to drink; for they are worthy.

7 And I heard another out of the altar say, Even so, Lord God Almighty, true and righteous are thy judgments.

Again we have fire sent upon water, heating it and evaporating it.

Revelation 8

12 And the fourth angel sounded, and the third part of the sun was smitten, and the third part of the moon, and the third part of the stars; so as the third part of them was darkened, and the day shone not for a third part of it, and the night likewise.

A feature is added by the parallel passage.

Revelation 16

8 And the fourth angel poured out his vial upon the sun; and power was given unto him to scorch men with fire.

9 And men were scorched with great heat, and blasphemed the name of God, which hath power over these plagues: and they repented not to give him glory.

Part of the time the sun is darkened; the rest of the time it shines with intense heat, so great that people are scorched as with fire. Never has the sun been that hot before.

These four plagues cover a period of about two years. The next two plagues cover a year and a half; then there is a period of three and a half years, during which there is no rain, so, for seven years water will be passing into the sky with very little, if any, returning to the earth. That, with the earthquakes that move mountains into the sea, would probably be sufficient to bring about the condition which John described when he said: "And there was no more sea."

This is the end of the program of redemption begun some 6,000 years ago; but it is not the end of the world or of the human race.

Revelation 21

3 And I heard a great voice out of heaven saying, Behold, the tabernacle of God is with men, and

he will dwell with them, and they shall be his people, and God himself shall be with them, and be their God.

4 And God shall wipe away all tears from their eyes; and there shall be no more death, neither sorrow, nor crying, neither shall there be any more pain: for the former things are passed away.

All people are invited to participate in this glorious new heaven and earth. Death is not a factor, for God will raise the dead.

Revelation 22
17 And the Spirit and the bride say, Come. And let him that heareth say, Come. And let him that is athirst come. And whosoever will, let him take the water of life freely.

You may be assured of your place, reserved in advance.

John 14
2 In my Father's house are many mansions: if it were not so, I would have told you. I go to prepare a place for you.

3 And if I go and prepare a place for you, I will come again, and receive you unto myself; that where I am, there ye may be also.

But there is only one way—through the door. Many other ways are offered. Many voices are raised to confuse. There are many false christs, and more are coming. Jesus said:

John 10
9 I am the door: by me if any man enter in, he shall be saved.

John 5
24 Verily, verily, I say unto you, He that heareth my word, and believeth on him that sent me, hath everlasting life, and shall not come into condemnation; but is passed from death unto life.